The
Essentials
of Grammar

Concise Guides
for the Next Century

The
Essentials
of Grammar

Compiled by

Hayden Mead, Ph.D.,
and Jay Stevenson, Ph.D.

Developed by The Philip Lief Group, Inc.

BERKLEY BOOKS, NEW YORK

THE ESSENTIALS OF GRAMMAR

A Berkley Book / published by arrangement with
The Philip Lief Group, Inc.

PRINTING HISTORY
Berkley edition / September 1996

The Putnam Berkley World Wide Web site address is
http://www.berkley.com

ISBN: 0-425-15446-7

BERKLEY®
Berkley Books are published by The Berkley Publishing Group,
200 Madison Avenue, New York, New York 10016.
BERKLEY and the "B" design
are trademarks belonging to Berkley Publishing Corporation.

PRINTED IN THE UNITED STATES OFF AMERICA

10 9 8 7 6 5 4 3 2 1

INTRODUCTION

This book is part of a series of authoritative reference wordbooks created for people of the 1990s who need to communicate effectively both in person and on paper, and who must find reliable answers quickly and efficiently. The definitions, principles, and examples presented in *The Essentials of Grammar* will provide writers with clear, comprehensive information in a revolutionary new way. Whether for writing or editing, this book successfully combines a dictionary format with dependable accuracy and authority. Unlike some overly dense manuals that tend to frustrate rather than instruct, *The Essentials of Grammar* presents essential information on grammar and usage in easy-to-understand language unburdened by technical jargon.

The Essentials of Grammar resolves the questions that writers of all levels ask. Whether you need to know when to use the past perfect progressive tense or find out the difference between *adverse* and *averse,* this book is the easiest reference guide available. Entries include simple explanations and numerous useful examples of proper and improper usage so that you can find answers with maximum ease and return to your keyboard as soon as possible. The book is also exhaustively cross-referenced for even easier access to information.

Invaluable for the student, teacher, office assistant,

writer, copy editor, editor, grammarian, and business writer, *The Essentials of Grammar* is a complete reference handbook for use whenever those prickly, seemingly unanswerable grammatical questions arise.

A

a, an, the

A, an, and **the** comprise the group of noun determiners known as articles. **A** and **an** are indefinite articles; **the** is a definite article. **A** is used when the following word begins with a consonant sound regardless of whether or not the first letter of that word is actually a consonant: *a hospital, a once-in-a-lifetime opportunity, a united front.* **An** is used when the following word begins with a vowel sound, regardless of whether or not the first letter of the word is actually a vowel: *an anteater, an S-shaped line, an hourglass.* Formerly, **an** was used before those words beginning with the letter **h** and having an unaccented first syllable, as in *an humongous error.* This rule has become obsolete.

A or **an** are indefinite articles and are used rather than **the** before a general noun when it is not known which specific thing is referred to, as in the sentence, *A ferret makes a good pet.* **The,** a definite article, is used before a specific noun: *the ferret next door is a nuisance.* When mentioning a thing for the first time, it is best to use **a** or **an** and subsequently to use **the** once that thing has been specified. *A cloud floated by . . . The cloud came to rest over Hackensack, New Jersey.*

Abbreviations

In formal writing, abbreviations for proper names, including the names of people, places, days, and months, are generally considered inappropriate. Abbreviations for units of measurement are acceptable in scientific and technical writing but not in other kinds of formal writing. Abbreviations of titles such as **Dr.** and **Ms.** are generally acceptable as are abbreviations of familiar countries, institutions, and organizations, such as **USA, AT&T,** and **AFL-CIO.** Latin abbreviations are appropriate for citations and notes. These include: **cf.** for confer (compare), **e.g.** for *exempli gratia* (for example); and **et al.** for *et alii* (and others).

ability of, to

Ability to do is preferable to **ability of doing,** as it is more direct.

able

Able should not be used as part of a passive construction. It is thus incorrect to say, *He was able to be drafted.* The sentence should read, *He could be drafted.*
   See also **PASSIVE VOICE.**

above

Above is sometimes used to refer to statements made previously in a piece of writing. *As argued above, dogwood trees are a public menace.* Such constructions should be used sparingly and only when **above** refers to a specific idea or passage. A gesture as general as **the above** should be avoided entirely.

Absolute phrases

An absolute phrase uses the verb form **-ed** or **-ing** and modifies an entire sentence. *The guests having departed, we were stuck with the dirty dishes.* Here, **the guests having departed** is an absolute phrase. An absolute phrase may be placed at the beginning or the end of a sentence. Absolute phrases can lend a sophisticated tone to one's speech or writing since they provide a way of joining two complete ideas without bothering with the uninteresting and often overused conjunction **and.** Some writers, however, have an unfortunate tendency to pad their discourse with absolute phrases containing the unnecessary word **being,** which adds nothing of substance and should be avoided. *The results being known, it is plain to see I have proved my point.* This sentence is devoid of useful information.

See also SENTENCE MODIFIERS.

Absolute terms

Absolute terms are words that identify characteristics that, strictly speaking, do not occur in differing degrees. These include **unique, perfect, whole, exact, dead, lost,** etc. Although it is not logically appropriate to speak of absolute terms in the context of comparisons such as **deader,** or **more whole,** or **less exact,** it is often convenient to do so. Some absolute terms may be used comparatively whereas others should not. Among the terms that, in general, should not be used comparatively are **unique** and **equal.**

Abstract language

As opposed to concrete language, abstract language refers to intangible concepts rather than to things that can be perceived by the senses. **Truth, happiness, treachery,** and **clarity** are abstract concepts. **Smoke, ball bearings, slime,** and **fingernails** are concrete terms. Abstractness and concreteness are both abstract concepts.

Abstract language is necessary in writing, especially in analytic prose. Because abstract terms are often more difficult to understand than concrete terms, it is important to use them with consistency and precision. Writers sometimes find it necessary to define certain abstract terms in special ways in order to make them useful in the specific contexts in which they are to be used. **Hope** or **kindness,** for example, are terms that may take on special meanings depending on how they are used. Deprived of a specific context, abstractions can be empty or vague.

See also CONCRETE LANGUAGE.

accept, except

Accept is a verb meaning to receive or believe something. *We accept our lot in life.* When used as a verb, **except** means to leave something out. *I excepted the expensive items from the shopping list.* More frequently, **except** is used as a preposition. *You can take any car you want except the blue one.* As a preposition, **except** should be used to refer to the object, not the subject, of a sentence. Thus it is incorrect to say, *Except for the children, we ate everything on our plates.*

acceptance, acceptation
Acceptance means **the act of receiving favorably or with equanimity.** *Their eventual acceptance of the bad news made things easier in the long run.* **Acceptation** means the way a word or expression is commonly understood. *"Awful" in its obsolete acceptation meant "amazing."*

accompanied by, accompanied with
People may be said to be **accompanied by** others. Things may be said to be **accompanied with** other things.

acquiesce
Acquiesce, a verb meaning **comply with** or **consent to,** takes the preposition **in.** *He acquiesced in my demands.* It is not appropriate to say **acquiesce with** or **acquiesce to.**

act, action
Act is generally used to refer to deeds performed by people or humanlike beings. The term emphasizes the result rather than the process of action. *The earthquake was an act of nature.* **Action** emphasizes the process rather than the result and refers to human as well as nonhuman behavior. *She cannot account for her actions.*

Active voice
In active voice, the subject of a sentence carries out the action referred to by the verb. *I ate the polliwog.* In passive voice, the subject is that which is acted upon. *I was sickened by my dinner.* In general, the passive voice is

less acceptable than the active voice, which is clearer and more direct. Thus the preceding example should be changed to read: *My dinner sickened me.* The passive voice, however, can be used effectively to emphasize the uncertain nature of the source of an action. *They will be cast into outer darkness where there is wailing and gnashing of teeth. A good time was had by all.*

See also **PASSIVE VOICE.**

adage

See also **OLD ADAGE.**

additionally

Additionally, the adverbial form of **additional** should be avoided, especially when used to refer to the process of providing further explanation or information. **Moreover** and **furthermore** are more suitable.

adduce, deduce, induce

Adduce means **use as an example** or **suggest for consideration.** *To bolster her claim that animals are more intelligent than people, she adduced that television advertising persuades people to buy things.* **Deduce** and **induce** both mean **conclude** or **infer. Deduce** means to draw conclusions about particular things based on general principles. **Induce** means to draw conclusions about general principles based on particular things. *Having witnessed his dislike for women, we deduced that he was unable to relate to his mother. We induced his dislike for women after hearing him complain about his female colleagues.*

Adjectives

Adjectives are parts of speech that modify nouns or pronouns. A kind of modifier, they may be contrasted with adverbs, which modify verbs, adjectives, and other adverbs. There are three kinds of adjectives: positive, comparative, and superlative. An adjective is positive when it simply describes the noun or pronoun. *The hungry spider.* Here **hungry** is an adjective modifying **spider.** An adjective is comparative when it relates two similar things. *My second toe is longer than my first.* Here **longer** is an adjective modifying **second toe** in relation to **my first.** An adjective may be superlative when it refers to an extreme. *That was the quietest shout I ever heard.* Here **quietest** is an adjective modifying **shout** in relation to all other shouts heard.

Although poets writing before the twentieth century often placed adjectives after nouns and pronouns— *"The elephant wreathed his long proboscis lithe."*— Milton—adjectives ordinarily come before the nouns and pronouns they modify: *The elephant wreathed his long, lithe proboscis.* Of course, adjectives can be piled on one after another, but more than two or three adjectives together tend to be humorous or peculiar rather than informative.

Adjectives are ordinarily thought of as individual words, but entire groups of words, called adjective clauses and adjective phrases, may function together as a single adjective. One way to make several words function as an adjective is to connect them with hyphens. *Our church is sponsoring an all-you-can-eat jellyfish breakfast. I'm tired of your why-is-everyone-always-picking-their-ears attitude.*

Another way to use a group of words as a single adjective is to put them in an adjective clause. An adjective clause is a kind of dependent clause that begins with **that, which, who, whom,** or **whose.** The clause generally comes after the word it modifies. *Your hair, which always dangles down into your soup, is your best feature.*

See also **ADVERBS; COMPARISON;** and **MODIFIERS.**

admission, admittance

Admission may be used to refer to the right to enter a specific place. *Admission is free on Tuesdays.* **Admittance** refers to the specific act of entering. *Your admittance without a ticket was an oversight.*

admit

It is unnecessary to use the preposition **to** with **admit.** It is sufficient to say, *I admit the error. I admit having made a mistake.*

adopted, adoptive

Children may be **adopted.** The parents adopting them are **adoptive.**

Adverbs

Adverbs are the parts of speech that modify verbs, adjectives, or other adverbs. Like adjectives, which modify nouns and pronouns, adverbs are modifiers. Also like adjectives, adverbs may be positive, comparative, and superlative and may consist of single words or of entire clauses.

Some adjectival forms of words are often used mistakenly as adverbs, such as *good, bad, sure,* and *real.*

When these words are used to modify verbs, the adverbial form should be used: *well, badly, surely,* and *really.*

Adverb forms are sometimes given to words that do not require them:

Improper Adverbs
Muchly, thusly, firstly, secondly, thirdly, and *importantly* when used as a sentence modifier

See also ADJECTIVES; COMPARISONS; MODIFIERS; and SENTENCE MODIFIERS.

adverse, averse

Adverse is an adjective meaning **unfavorable** and it is used to refer to circumstances. *The adverse weather ruined our vacation.* **Averse** is an adjective meaning **opposed** and is used to refer to people. *We are averse to the growing of dogwoods on public property.*

advice, advise

Advice is the noun form of the verb **to advise.** *Take my advice; I advise you.*

affect, effect

Affect means to influence; **effect,** as a verb, means to bring about. More commonly, **effect** is used as a noun meaning result. *My complaints did not affect his decision. They did not effect a change in plan. They did not produce the effect I desired.*

affinity

Affinity should not be followed by the preposition **for.** The appropriate preposition is usually **with** and some-

times **of** or **between.** *I have an affinity with older people. An affinity of Alabamians has developed. There is
an affinity between me and my couch.*

agenda, agendas, agendum

Agenda is a collective, plural noun meaning **set of
goals. Agendas** may be used to designate more than one
agenda. **Agendum** may be used to mean **single thing to
be done.** *My first agenda is to keep the house clean. It
conflicts with the agendas of relaxing, improving my
mind, and meeting people. My next agendum is to iron
my shirts.*

aggravate, irritate

Although **aggravate** and **irritate** are often used interchangeably, **aggravate,** strictly speaking, means **make
worse** and thus should only be used to refer to problems
that exist prior to aggravation. **Irritate** may be used to
mean **annoy.**

ago that, ago since

Ago since is redundant and incorrect. When a dependent clause is used to modify **ago, that** is the appropriate relative pronoun to use. *It was a week ago that I first
felt back pain.* It is preferable to omit the dependant
clause altogether. *I first felt back pain a week ago.*

See also **DEPENDENT CLAUSES**, **REDUNDANCY**, and
RELATIVE PRONOUNS.

Agreement

Words with forms that vary according to number, person, and gender must agree or correspond with one another so that number, person, and gender remain

consistent. Those parts of speech that must agree are subjects with verbs and pronouns with antecedents.

> ### Faulty Agreement: Subject-Verb
> *I considers, you exclaims, she possess, they disintegrates, we prefers*

> ### Correct Agreement: Subject-Verb
> *I eliminate, you condone, he establishes, they elevate, we conceive*

Note that special subject-verb agreement problems are posed by sentences that use collective nouns as subjects:

> ### Faulty Agreement: Collective Noun-Verb
> *Nothing are, the batch are done, the group decide*

> ### Correct Agreement: Collective Noun-Verb
> *The committee thinks, the herd stampedes, all members of the group decide*

> ### Faulty Agreement: Pronoun-Antecedent
> **Each** *of us has* **their** *own bazooka.* **All** *of us believe in* **herself.** **Everyone** *is as young as* **they** *feel.*

> ### Correct Agreement: Pronoun-Antecedent
> **Some** *of us think before* **we** *speak.* **One** *should appreciate* **her** *friends.* **All** *of us take care of* **ourselves.**

See also **COLLECTIVE NOUNS**; **PRONOUN-REFERENCE**; AND **SUBJECT-VERB AGREEMENT**.

ain't
This is a nonstandard contraction meaning **am not, are not, is not,** etc. It is usually considered unacceptable in formal writing.

all, all of
All of may be used with personal pronouns, but otherwise, all should not take the preposition of. *I know all of you. You planted all the dogwoods on Main Street.*

all are, all is
All is an indefinite pronoun that functions as a collective noun. It can take either a plural or singular verb. In terms of placement, both all are and are all are correct. *They all are dizzy. It all looks funny.* If all is used to refer to people, the verb should be plural.

See also COLLECTIVE NOUNS.

all ready, already
All ready is an adjective phrase meaning prepared used to modify nouns. *The dogwoods are all ready for pruning.* Already is an adverb meaning prior to this moment used to modify verbs. *We have already ensured their safety.*

all right, alright
All right is casual and should be avoided in formal writing. Alright is nonstandard and should be avoided even in casual writing.

all together, altogether
All together may be used to refer to a coherent group. *Your foods are mixed all together in your stomach.* Altogether means entirely. *Your continual references to bodily processes are altogether inappropriate.*

allude, elude, refer

Allude is similar to **refer,** but is less direct. *The natives made gestures with their hands to allude to our funny hats.* **Elude** means **avoid** or **escape,** but suggests a planned evasive procedure. *They tried to follow us, but we eluded them.*

allusion, illusion

An allusion is an unexplicit reference to something. An illusion is a misleading appearance. *He mentioned the old illusion of the woman being sawed in half as an allusion to Houdini, the famous magician.*

almost, most

Almost is an adverb or adjective meaning **nearly. Most** is an adjective meaning **a majority of.** It is sometimes used colloquially in place of **almost,** but such usage is nonstandard. It is thus incorrect to say, *The ballet is most over.*

alongside of

The preposition **of** is unnecessary with **alongside** and should be omitted. *Dogwoods grew alongside the fence.* **Alongside** should not be used unless the dimension of length is involved. Otherwise use **beside.** *A dogwood grew beside the fence.*

a lot, alot, allot

A lot is a collective noun meaning many. The commonly used word **alot** is incorrect. The unrelated word **allot** means to distribute or share as a portion.

See also **COLLECTIVE NOUNS.**

already, all ready

See also ALL READY, ALREADY.

alright, all right

See also ALL RIGHT, ALRIGHT.

alumna, alumnus, alumni

An **alumna** is a female graduate. An **alumnus** is a male graduate. **Alumni,** the masculine plural form, is often used generically for groups consisting of more than one alumna and/or alumnus. Casually, **alums** may be used as the plural form. **Alumnae** is the feminine plural form.

See also GENERIC HE.

Ambiguity

An ambiguity is a statement that seems to have more than one meaning. Ambiguity often results unintentionally from poor grammatical construction. *Discarded pieces of food are unsightly and attract rats. They are our biggest problem.* Here the vague reference of the pronoun, they, creates ambiguity. It is unclear whether rats or discarded food pose the biggest problem. Clearer pronoun reference would eliminate this ambiguity.

See also PRONOUN REFERENCE.

amiable, amicable

Both **amiable** and **amicable** mean **pleasant** or **agreeable,** but **amiable** refers only to people. *He seemed amiable until I realized he had stolen my wallet.* **Amicable** refers only to situations. *We had an amicable relationship until he stole my wallet.*

among, between
Among refers to a situation concerning three or more things. **Between** concerns two things. *We divided the loot among the three of us. I had to choose between the gold watch and the tape recorder.*

amoral, immoral
Both **amoral** and **immoral** mean **not moral,** but **amoral** means **lacking morals of any kind, good or bad,** whereas **immoral** means **having bad morals.** Thus animals may be considered amoral, but only humans may be immoral.

amount, number
Amount refers to an abstract quantity or mass that cannot be counted. **Number** refers to specific, countable things. Nouns that have amount rather than number are collective nouns. They generally take singular verb forms, but often take plural verbs as well. Nouns that have number are count nouns. They take plural verb forms when they are plural. In English, any amount of hair is usually considered too great a number of hairs to be counted. Thus **hair** is usually used as a collective noun and is thought to have amount rather than number. *Your hair is falling into your soup.* Here, **hair** is regarded as a singular collective noun and takes a singular verb. Nevertheless, hairs are countable and may be thought of as a number rather than an amount. *Three hairs are growing out of this mole.* Here, **hairs** is a plural count noun and takes a plural verb.

See also COLLECTIVE NOUNS and COUNT NOUNS.

Amounts

When numerical amounts are used as subjects of a sentence, the sentence takes a singular verb. *Eight beers is a lot to drink in one night.*

Ampersand

An ampersand is the symbol **&** which is a shorthand designation meaning **and.** It is useful in taking notes and can be seen in business names, but should be avoided in formal writing.

and

And is a common conjunction meaning **together with,** used to join equivalent elements. It is often considered inappropriate to begin a sentence with **and,** although doing so can sometimes effectively emphasize a point. More often, however, beginning a sentence with **and** is an imprecise, lazy, or redundant means of relating ideas. *Reptiles are cold-blooded creatures that lay eggs. And they are nearly fully developed at birth.* Here the logical relationship between egg-laying and development at birth is obscured by the **and,** which suggests the two characteristics are equal and independent rather than interdependent. The sentence might be revised to read, *Because they are cold blooded creatures that lay eggs, reptiles are nearly fully developed at birth.*

See also CONJUNCTIONS and COORDINATION.

and/or

The words **and** and **or** joined by a slash present a choice among three possibilities: either or both of two alternatives. *All passengers under four feet tall and/or under eight years of age may ride free.*

another

Another should be used to indicate a single additional thing, but not a number of things. It is thus incorrect to say, *They poisoned another seven dogwoods last night.* This sentence should read, *They poisoned an additional seven dogwoods.*

antagonist, protagonist

Antagonist may mean **enemy** or **villain in a work of fiction. Protagonist** means **main character in a work of fiction.** These terms should not be used to describe real people.

ante, anti

Ante and **anti** are both prefixes. **Ante** means **before** as in **antebellum** and **antecedent. Anti** means **against** as in **antiseptic** and **antigovernment.**

Antecedents

An antecedent is the noun to which a pronoun refers. *I received the guacamole, for which I thank you.* Here **guacamole** is the antecedent of the pronoun, **which.**

A singular pronoun requires a singular antecedent; a plural pronoun requires a plural antecedent. *A frog will rarely jump as far as it can. Frogs tend to be lazy unless they are swimming.* Here **it** refers to the singular antecedent, **frog** and **they** refers to the plural antecedent, **frogs.**

Traditionally, the male pronoun **he** has been used along with indefinite pronouns **everybody, everyone,**

somebody, someone, etc., regardless of whether or not women were being referred to. *Everyone should love his country.* Recently, this has come to be considered biased, or noninclusive language. Some alternatives are, *Everyone should love her country,* or *Everyone should love his or her country,* or *All people should love their country.*

> *Faulty Agreement: Pronoun-Antecedent*
> ***Each*** *of us has* ***their*** *own bazooka.* ***All*** *of us believe in* ***herself.*** *Everyone is as young as* ***they*** *feel.*

> *Correct Agreement: Pronoun-Antecedent*
> ***Some*** *of us think before we speak.* ***One*** *should appreciate* ***her*** *friends.* ***All*** *of us take care of* ***ourselves.***

See also **AGREEMENT, BIASED LANGUAGE,** and **IN-DEFINITE PRONOUNS.**

any are, any is

Any is an indefinite pronoun that functions as a collective noun and may be used with either a plural or a singular verb. *Any donations are appreciated. Any time is the right time.*

See also **COLLECTIVE NOUNS.**

any more

Any more is properly an indefinite pronoun, but it is sometimes used colloquially as an adverb meaning **currently.** *There are no dogwoods left any more.* This usage is nonstandard and should be avoided. It is more appropriate to say, *There are no more dogwoods left,* or, *There aren't any more dogwoods.*

anyone, any one

Anyone refers to any unspecified person; **any one** means a specific person or thing belonging to a particular group. *Anyone who can talk can sing. Any one of those buttons will look fine.*

anyways, anywheres

These terms are nonstandard variants of the adverbs, **anyway** and **anywhere. Anyways** and **anywheres** are both considered unacceptable. The **s** is usually unnecessary after such adverbs as **anyway, anywhere, somewhere,** and **alongside.** An exception to this rule is **besides,** which requires the **s** to distinguish it from the preposition, **beside.**

See also BESIDE, BESIDES.

apogee, perigee

Literally, **apogee** refers to the farthest point from the earth of the moon's orbit; perigee to the closest point. Figuratively, **apogee** means **best moment in a period of time.** *The careers of most professional athletes reach their apogee early.* **Perigee,** used figuratively, means the worst moment or lowest point.

See also FIGURATIVE LANGUAGE and LITERAL LANGUAGE.

Apostrophes

An apostrophe is a punctuation mark (') used to show possession and used in contractions. For possessives, **'s** may be added to the end of a word unless the word is a plural ending in **s,** in which case only the apostrophe is added. *A dog's life. Our cities' decline.* For singular words ending in s, use **'s**. *A kiss's taste.* Apostrophes may be used in contractions to indicate where one or more letters have been omitted: **don't, can't,** etc. Contractions should be avoided in formal writing.

See also **CONTRACTIONS** and **POSSESSIVE CASE.**

Appositives

An appositive is a phrase that is not a necessary part of a sentence but explains or identifies a noun. It appears directly after the noun it modifies. *Prosthesis, the science of artificial body parts, improves the lives of millions.* Here the phrase, **the science of artificial body parts,** is an appositive.

See also **PHRASES.**

appraise, apprise, assess

Appraise and **assess** both mean **evaluate,** but **appraise** has a much more specific meaning: **ascribe a monetary value to.** *I'm having my bottle cap collection appraised.* **Assess** means more generally **to consider and form a judgment.** *After assessing the market, I've decided not to sell my bottle caps.* **Apprise** means **inform** and is generally used in regard to ongoing situations. *Let me apprise you of my efforts to open a bottle cap museum.*

apprehend, comprehend

Both **apprehend** and **comprehend** mean **understand,** but **apprehend** suggests a more intuitive reaching out with the mind while **comprehend** indicates a firm grasp of an idea. *It has taken some time to apprehend your spiritual beliefs. Religious faith involves belief in things we cannot comprehend.*

a priori, prima facie

A priori is a term borrowed from Latin used to refer to conclusions. It means **based on conventional wisdom rather than on experience. A priori** is sometimes confused with **prima facie,** which may also be used to refer to conclusions and means **on first glance.** *She decided, a priori, that she wanted to go out with him, but realized, prima facie, that she did not like him.*

apt, likely, liable

Apt may be used to refer to a personal or natural tendency. *She is apt to become silly when she is tired.* **Likely** may be used to refer to matters of mere probability. *It is likely to rain tomorrow.* **Liable** should not be used to refer to mere probability but may be used to suggest the likelihood of an undesirable outcome. *You are liable to slip if you wear those shoes.*

arbitrate, mediate

Arbitrate means **decide on a course of action after listening to the recommendations of all interested parties.** *The teachers' dispute with the board of education was so serious that the government had to arbitrate a new contract.* **Mediate** means **help conflicting sides reach an agreement.** *We hoped that if Reverend Phelps mediated the dispute, it would not need to go into arbitration.*

aren't I

Aren't I is a nonstandard version of **am I not** and should be avoided in formal discourse.

Argument

The argument of a piece of expository writing is its thesis and the evidence used to support it. This evidence
may include not only ideas attributed to other writers,
but demonstrations of the limitations of contradicting
views. Indeed, presenting both sides of a debate can be
an especially persuasive and productive way to build an
argument.

See also **THESIS.**

Articles

A type of noun determiner, articles consist of the definite article, **the,** and the indefinite articles **a** and **an.**

See also **A, AN, THE.**

as . . . as, so . . . as

In formal writing, **as . . . as** comparisons are reserved
for positive examples; **so . . . as** should be used to make
negative comparisons. *I am as hungry as I have ever
been, but not so hungry as Edmund is usually.*

as, like

As and **like** are two commonly misused prepositions.
As means serving the purpose of. *I use a fossil as a pa-
perweight.* **Like** means similarly to. *He eats like a
horse.*

Like is often used colloquially in place of **as,** which
can sound overformal. *Act like a man.*

As should be used to indicate a specific role or function. It is misleading and vague to say, *I respect her as a
person,* since, logically, there is no alternative. **As** should

also be used rather than **like** when giving examples. *I enjoy important writers such as Margaret Cavendish.*

as follows

As follows may be used whether or not what comes next is plural or singular. *The recommendations are as follows.* It is unacceptable to say **as follow.**

assess, appraise, apprise

See also APPRAISE, APPRISE, ASSESS.

assume, presume

Assume and **presume** both mean **accept as true.** In general, assumptions are more justified than presumptions, which may involve social impropriety as well as factual uncertainty. *I assume you are new here or you would not have presumed to sit on the Fabergé egg.*

assure, ensure, insure

To assure is to convince or promise a person. To ensure is to make an event certain. To insure is to make a contract to pay for losses. *My dream assured me that I was asleep. To ensure my sleep, I took some pills. My pension plan insures the cost of the medicine.*

Asterisk

An asterisk (*) is a symbol that is generally used to refer the reader to a footnote. Asterisks may be used instead of numbered footnotes if there are only a couple of them.

at about

At about is often used colloquially to mean **approximately.** *I get off work at about 3* A.M. **Approximately** should be used in formal writing.

Attribution

Attribution refers to the way writers indicate that the ideas and assumptions they describe are not their own. Attribution includes, but is not limited to, quotation and citation. In addition, writers may attribute ideas and assumptions to others whom they neither quote nor cite as, for example, a way of thinking that an entire group of people share.

Attribution provides an important means of framing or contextualizing a writer's ideas. Ideas may be recognized as important or original only in the context of other ideas belonging to other people. Thus, in order to demonstrate the significance of an idea, a writer must show how it relates to other ideas.

Attribution is necessary when demonstrating new uses for old ideas and when showing weaknesses and limitations in old ideas. Such reference to old ideas is necessary in order to show that the writer's ideas are, in contrast, new.

See also **CITATION; CONTEXT; ORIGINALITY;** and **QUOTATIONS.**

Attributive adjective

An attributive adjective, as opposed to a predicate adjective, modifies a noun that directly precedes or follows it. An example is the word **contagious** in the phrase, **contagious disease.**

See also **PREDICATE ADJECTIVE.**

Attributive noun
An attributive noun is a noun used as an adjective. An example is the word **piano** in the phrase **piano player.**

augment, enhance
Augment refers to quantity; **enhance** refers to quality. Thus **augment** means **make bigger** or **make more numerous.** *We enlisted some inexperienced players simply to augment the size of our team.* **Enhance** means **improve** or **make better.** *Experienced players would have enhanced our team's performance.*

Auxiliary verbs
Also called a helping verb, an auxiliary verb is combined with a main verb to create progressive tenses, perfect tenses, and the passive voice, as well as to emphasize, question, or negate.

The progressive tense of the main verb, **sneeze,** can be made by adding **-ing** and preceding an auxiliary verb such as **is,** or **has been**: *She has been sneezing.*

The perfect tense of the main verb, **to scratch,** is made by adding **-ed** and preceding an auxiliary verb such as **had, have,** or **will have:** *I will have scratched by the time you bring the lotion.*

The passive voice is made when a form of the verb, **to be** is used as an auxiliary verb. *I am astonished by your candor.* Here **am** is an auxiliary of the main verb, **astonished.**

A form of the verb, **to do** can be used as an auxiliary verb in order to emphasize or negate assertions or to put them as questions. *I did squash the pomegranate! I did not feel remorse. Do you think I lack fortitude?*

See also **PASSIVE VOICE; PERFECT TENSES;** and **PROGRESSIVE TENSES.**

avenge, revenge

Both **avenge** and **revenge** refer to vindication, but **avenge** is more general. **Avenge** may be used to refer to any punitive response to injury or insult, whereas **revenge** refers to one's own response to a personal grievance. You can avenge another's wrong, but strictly speaking you can revenge only yourself.

averse, adverse

See also **ADVERSE, AVERSE.**

avert, avoid, prevent

Avert means **turn aside** and is usually used to refer to consequences of events, although one may also avert one's eyes. *I averted a collision by driving off the road.*

Avoid means **turn away from** and may refer to people and things as well as abstractions. *She avoided him by ducking into a crowded store.*

Both **avert** and **avoid** are generally used in regard to circumstances that are immediately present. **Prevent** is used in regard to circumstances that are not immediately present. *I prevent theft by keeping my bottle cap collection under lock and key.*

awake, awaken, wake, waken

Any of these forms are acceptable in formal discourse. Acceptable past tense forms are **awaked, waked, awakened, wakened, awoke,** or **woke.** The past tense forms **awoked** and **woked** are nonstandard and inappropriate in formal writing.

awful, awfully

Awful is an adjective meaning **extremely bad. Awful** and **awfully** are also used in colloquial speech as intensifying adverbs, as in the phrases **awful big** and **awfully nice.** Neither **awful** nor **awfully** should be used as intensifiers in formal writing. Even in its proper sense, **awful** should be used sparingly in formal discourse. Its chief use is as a value judgment; it adds no specific information about the nouns it modifies.

a while, awhile

A while is a noun. **Awhile** is an adverbial form of the noun. In many sentences, it is unclear whether a noun or an adverb is intended, as in **stay a while/awhile.** In such cases, either **a while** or **awhile** is acceptable. Although it is unnecessary, the preposition **for** may be used with **a while,** but should not be used with **awhile.**

B

Back-formation

A back-formation is a word that originates as the supposed root word of a word that existed first. An example is the verb **laze,** which is a false root of the adjective, **lazy.** Many back-formations have become acceptable terms in standard English. Some are not acceptable. Back-formations to avoid include **enthuse** and **emote.** Acceptable back-formations are **burgle** and **laze.**

bad, badly

Bad is an adjective; **badly,** an adverb. Thus **bad** should not be used to modify a verb. It is incorrect to say *I cook bad.* **Bad,** however, may be used as a subject complement after a linking verb in such sentences as *I sound bad,* or, *I feel bad,* or *I look bad,* etc.

See also LINKING VERBS and SUBJECT COMPLEMENTS.

because

See also REASON BECAUSE, REASON WHY.

before, preparatory to

Although **before** often implies a causal, in addition to a temporal, relationship, it does not, strictly speaking, show any logical connection between two events. *I* *stopped at the store before coming over. I had no intention, however, of getting you anything.* **Preparatory to,** although cumbersome, necessarily refers to a logical connection between events. *I stopped off at the store preparatory to coming over in order to buy you some doilies.* **Preparatory to** should not be used instead of before when there is no causal relationship.

behalf

In behalf of means **for the benefit of.** *The pig roast is held in behalf of the volunteer fire department.* **On behalf of** means **acting on the part of.** *I accept this award on behalf of my wife who could not be present.* The plural form of **behalf** is **behalfs.** This plural form is only necessary where two behalfs are different. *My parents are so antagonistic that it is impossible to do any one thing in their respective behalfs.*

being as, being that

Being as and **being that** are nonstandard terms meaning **because** or **since.** They introduce absolute phrases in a way that is generally considered unacceptable. *Being that the wind was blowing, we decided to fly our kites.* This sentence should read, *Because the wind was blowing, we decided to fly our kites.*

See also **ABSOLUTE PHRASES.**

beside, besides

Beside is a preposition; **besides** is an adverb. **Beside** means next to; **besides** means instead of. Whereas the **s** on the end of **besides** is necessary to distinguish it from the word meaning **next to,** there are several words to which an **s** is sometimes added unnecessarily, such as

towards, aways, and **somewheres.** Of these examples, only **towards** is acceptable, although **toward** is preferred.

better than, more than
Better than is sometimes used colloquially as a synonym for **more than.** *I have better than a thousand bottle caps in my collection.* Such usage should be avoided in formal writing.

between, among
See also AMONG, BETWEEN.

between you and I, me
The phrase **between you and I** is incorrect since it is an adverbial phrase that requires the object case pronoun, **me.**
See also CASE.

bi, semi
Bi is a prefix meaning **two** or **twice.** When used in words such as **biweekly** or **bimonthly** it means **every two weeks or months.** Thus a biweekly publication comes out once every two weeks. **Semi** means **half.** A semiweekly publication comes out twice a week. **Bi,** however, does not always indicate that an event occurs once in two periods of time. Although **biyearly** means **once every two years,** and **semiyearly** means **twice a year, biannually** means **twice a year. Biennially** means **once in two years.**

Biased language

While many biased terms are obvious signs of bigotry
and need no comment here, some terms such as **Ne-
groes** and **ladies,** considered polite in previous decades,
are now considered offensive because they have been
used so frequently during eras when inequality was
widely condoned. Most readers today find **women** the
most appropriate means of designating human females
and **Blacks** a suitable way of referring to Negroid people, although many blacks prefer **African-American.**

Some words have become outmoded because they re-
flect biased attitudes. Moreover, the grammatical structure of language itself is changing to correct biases
reflected in the logic of that structure. Black English is
becoming recognized as a distinct dialect with its own
rules of grammar and usage rather than as simply a
"mistaken" or "incorrect" way of speaking. The use of
the pronoun **he** as generic to refer to individuals that
may be either male or female is now less acceptable
than the alternatives, **he or she** and **he/she.**

See also BLACK ENGLISH and INCLUSIVE LANGUAGE.

bit, bitten

Bitten, not **bit,** is properly the past participle of the verb
bite. *I didn't expect to be bitten on our first date.*

See also PARTICIPLES.

Black English

Many schools now recognize Black-American English
not as erroneous standard English, but as a distinct dialect with its own rules of grammar. Characteristics of
Black English is its different rules for subject-verb

agreement **he say, she believe,** the absence of helping verbs **we going,** subjunctive form helping verbs **they be hoping,** and the absence of the possessive case **my sister house** or **they red bicycle.** In spite of the fact that Black English has its own rules, many black students grow up learning that the language they have spoken from infancy is erroneous and that what sounds correct to them is mistaken, since their grammar is judged against standard English rather than on its own terms. Often without realizing it, these students are faced with the task of learning a different dialect. Because they and their teachers may not recognize that they need to learn a whole new set of grammatical rules in addition to the grammar they have already learned to hear, they may become frustrated or disgusted with repeatedly being told that they are wrong whenever they use their own dialect. In contrast, nonnative students of English grammar who have a more realistic sense of the difficulty of the task that faces them often learn with more self-confidence.

Sadly, howsoever Black English may be regarded in the classroom, it is commonly denigrated in the workplace. Studies have shown that potential employers have found applications and cover letters written in Black English to contain especially noticeable and unacceptable errors, even though they often fail to notice egregious mistakes not consistent with Black English in letters written by others. Because Black English is often confused with mistaken English, it is necessary that those who take just pride and pleasure in their command of standard English not use grammatical "correctness" as a tool of discrimination. Indeed, snobbery and ostentation often result in vague, unnecessarily complex writing that is far less clear and excusable than colloquial variants.

blatant, flagrant

Blatant means extremely obvious. It does not necessarily refer to a violation of rules as does **flagrant.** *In his blatant disregard for good manners, he grasped the teacup with both hands and drank it off in one gulp.* **Flagrant** refers to the obvious and usually deliberate violation of a rule. *The flag-burning was considered a flagrant violation of a state law.*

bore, born, borne

Bore is the past tense form of the verb **bear. Born** and **borne** are both past participles of **bear** in the sense of **give birth to. Borne** may be used to refer to the action of the bearer. **Borne** takes the preposition **by.** *I was borne by a very young woman.* When the action of the bearer giving birth is not at issue, the proper term is **born,** which takes the preposition **to.** *I was born to very young parents.* **Borne** may also be used to mean **carried.** *We have borne our troubles long enough.* **Born** should not be used to mean **carried.**

both

Both should only be used to refer to two things, not three or more. Thus it is incorrect to say **both index, middle, and ring fingers.**

Both should not be used with **alike, equally,** or **together.** It is redundant to say, *Both are equally good.*

See also **REDUNDANCY.**

Brackets

Brackets [ ] can be used to identify words that have been added to a direct quotation. *"Never give a [circus-going] sucker an even break."*—P. T. Barnum.

bring, take

Bring should be used to refer to the action of carrying something from a greater to a lesser distance away. *Bring home some ball bearings.* **Take** should be used to refer to the action of carrying something farther away. *Take these ball bearings to your sister.*

British spelling

Due largely to Noah Webster's influential efforts to reform American spelling, many word are spelled differently in England and America. Several abstract nouns that end in **or** in American spelling end in **our** in British, including **colour, behavior,** and **rumour.** Some nouns that end **er** in American spelling end **re** in British, including **theatre, centre,** and **metre.** Many verbs ending in **ize** or **yze** in American spelling are spelled to end **ise** or **yse** in England, including **apologise** and **analyse.** British spelling often requires an extra consonant before words ending in **ed, or,** and **ing** whereas American pelling does not. Some examples are **cancelled, councillor,** and **travelling.** Other words spelled differently in England and America are **anaemia/anemia, cheque/check, aluminium/aluminum, programme/ program,** and **waggon/wagon.**

broke, broken

Broke should not be used as the past participle of **break.** The proper form is broken. *The TV has been broken ever since the grammy awards.*

burglary, robbery

A burglary refers specifically to a theft that takes place in someone's home when no one is around. A robbery refers to a theft that takes place while the victims are actually present.

C

callus, callous

A **callus** is a patch of hardened skin caused by repeated chafing over a period of time. *She spends so much time looking through the keyhole that she has a callus on her nose where it rubs against the doorknob.*

Callous is an adjective meaning **hardhearted** or **unfeeling.** *His mother seemed callous about the death of his pet tarantula.* The suffix **-ous,** indicates that a word is an adjective.

can, may

Can and **may** are auxiliary verbs that are often confused with one another. **Can** means to be able; **may** means **possibly** or **to have permission.**

See also AUXILIARY VERBS.

cancel out

Cancel does not require the preposition **out,** which is redundant and should be omitted.

See also REDUNDANCY.

capital, capitol

A **capital** is a place, such as a city, where a government is located. A **capitol** is a building in which the chief government offices are located.

Capital letters

Capitals are used for the first letter of the first word of a sentence, of a proper noun, and of titles of people and works.

careen, career

Traditionally, writers have observed a distinction between **career** and **careen** when used as verbs. **Careen** could be used to mean **lean** or **tilt** whereas **career** could be used to mean **move rapidly and without control**. This distinction is no longer observed and now both **career** and **careen** may be used to refer to headlong movement.

Case

Nouns and pronouns take different forms depending on the function they serve within a sentence. These forms are called cases. There are three cases in standard English, the subjective or nominative case, the objective case, and the possessive case. All nouns and pronouns that are the subject of a sentence—that which carries out the action indicated by the verb—take the subjective case. In the sentence, *The dog chewed through its leash*, **dog** is the subject, **leash** the object, and **its** is a pronoun in the possessive case.

Personal pronouns in the subjective case are **I, you, she, he, it, we, they,** and **who.** Personal pronouns in the objective case are **me, you, her, him, it, us, them,** and **whom.** Possessive personal pronouns are **my** or **mine, your** or **yours, her** or **hers, his, its, our** or **ours, their** or **theirs,** and **whose.**

In most sentences, the subject comes before the object. As a result, many assume that the first noun or pronoun in a sentence should take the subjective case and the second noun or pronoun should take the objective case. This is erroneous in sentences in which the object comes before the subject. The following sentence, for example, misapplies the objective case to the subject: *The best dancer among us is him.* The sentence should read, *The best dancer is he,* or *He is the best dancer.*

Faulty Case
*There is Avery, **whom** is a good carpenter. The only hard worker is **her**. I don't like television as much as **them**. I'm going with **she**.*

Correct Case
*With **whom** will you be dancing? No one is nicer than **we**. I practice more than **they**.*

See also PRONOUNS.

celebrant, celebrator
Celebrant is restricted in meaning to **one who participates in a religious ritual.** Celebrator may be used more generally to refer to anyone who participates in festivities.

center on, center around
The phrase **center around** should be avoided. Instead, **revolve around** or **center on** may be used.

ceremonial, ceremonious
Ceremonial may be used as an adjective to describe any event that is like a ceremony. *A ceremonial gathering formed around the injured child.* **Ceremonious** may be used as an adjective to describe a manner, attitude, or

a person who has such an attitude. *He ushered us in with a ceremonious gesture.*

childish, childlike

To be childish is to resemble a child in an unappealing way by being selfish, unreasonable, inconsiderate, or ignorant. To be childlike is to resemble a child in an appealing way by being unprepossessing, sweet, gentle, or innocent.

children's, childrens'

Because **children** is plural, the apostrophe to show possession should come before the **s**. It is erroneous to write **childrens'**.

choice

Choice may be used to refer to the act of choosing and to things that are chosen. **Choice** is often used imprecisely to refer to options that may or may not be chosen. It is inaccurate to say *I have three choices,* if what is meant is, *I have a choice among three options.*

Citation

Citation is the act of quoting a written source as well as the act of documenting the source. Sources may be documented parenthetically as part of the text, in footnotes, in endnotes, or in works cited lists.

See also **QUOTATIONS.**

claim, declare

Although **claim** and **declare** are often used interchangeably, claim properly has a more specific meaning, **declare to own** or **declare rights to.** Declare should be used instead of claim when right or ownership is not involved. Thus it is imprecise to say, *He claimed that there are undiscovered craters on the moon.* It is appropriate, however, to say *He claimed the undiscovered craters on the moon as his.*

classic, classical

Classical means **having to do with antiquity, especially Greek and Roman art and the arts derived from them, or similar to them in spirit.** *She paints in something of a classical manner.* **Classic** may be used interchangeably with **classical** in this sense, but also may be used to refer to any excellent representation of its kind. *The whoopie cushion is a classic practical joke.*

Clauses

A clause is a grammatical construction that includes a subject and a verb. A sentence may be made up of one or more clauses. Understanding different kinds of clauses can be useful in determining where to place commas and in adding variety to sentence structure. The most important kinds of clauses are independent, also called main, and dependent, also called subordinate.

An independent clause can be a complete sentence on its own, requiring no further information to make it a complete thought. *The creature from outer space mowed down everything in its path.* An independent clause may also be combined with other independent clauses: *The creature from outer space mowed down everything in its path, but we finally stopped it by playing Neil Sedaka records,* or with dependent clauses, *The creature from outer space, although it appeared friendly, mowed down everything in its path.*

Dependent clauses require additional information to make them complete sentences, although, like other clauses, they have their own subject and verb. Dependent clauses can be adjective clauses, serving to modify the subject of an independent clause, or adverb clauses, modifying the verb of an independent clause. Adjective clauses begin with **that, which, who, whom,** or **whose.** These words are pronouns that refer to nouns used as the subjects of independent clauses. *The creature from outer space, whose body odor made us laugh, could juggle motorcycle tires with its three tongues.* Note that clauses may be divided by other clauses. In the preceding example, the independent clause is divided by the dependent clause. The dependent clause in this case is known as an embedded clause.

Some adjective clauses are known as essential clauses because they contain information that is necessary in order for the sentence to make sense. *Everyone who has three tongues may now eat the parking garage.* Since only those with three tongues may eat the garage, the clause, **who has three tongues** is essential. Without it, the sentence would be misleading. Essential clauses should not be separated from the rest of the sentence by commas. Nonessential clauses require commas to separate them.

Adverb clauses modify other verbs, adverbs, or adjectives. They may start with any of a variety of words including **although, as, because, before, even, if, since, though, unless, what, when,** and **while.** *Before it reached our planet, the creature from outer space was* *salivating.* The adverb clause beginning this sentence modifies the verb, **was salivating,** by telling when the action occurred. It is therefore an adverb clause.

If a sentence begins with a dependent clause, a comma should be placed after it and before the independent clause. If a sentence begins with an independent clause, no comma is necessary. *The creature from outer space was salivating before it reached our planet.* Compare this sentence, which begins with an independent clause, with the previous example, which begins with a dependent clause and hence requires a comma.

See also DEPENDENT CLAUSES; EMBEDDED CLAUSES; ESSENTIAL CLAUSES AND PHRASES; INDEPENDENT CLAUSES; and SENTENCES.

clench, clinch

Clench and **clinch** both mean **grasp or fasten securely.** **Clinch,** unlike **clench,** may also be used in a figurative sense, as in clinching an agreement or a victory.

See also FIGURATIVE LANGUAGE.

Clichés

Clichés are trite, commonplace expressions that should generally be avoided. *Don't count your chickens before they're hatched. I'll buy that for a dollar. And if you believe that, let me sell you the George Washington Bridge. You can say that again. Every dog has his day. Honesty is the best policy. Live and learn. Easy does it. He was fit to be tied. Time heals all wounds. One good turn deserves another. That's the way the cookie crumbles.*

climatic, climactic

Climatic is an adjective, the noun form of which is climate. Thus it means **having to do with regional meteorological conditions.** *I don't mind adverse climatic conditions.* Climactic is an adjective, the noun form of which is climax. It means **uppermost, most intense,** or **most extreme.** *The climactic moment of the play was when Billy traded in his peashooter for an assault rifle.*

close proximity

Proximity is a noun meaning **closeness.** Thus the phrase **close proximity** is redundant and should be avoided.

Collective nouns

Collective nouns refer to groups of things or people. Some collective nouns are **batch, herd, gang,** and **committee.** Collective nouns can be thought of as singular entities. In general, they agree with singular verb forms and singular pronouns. *The organization was careful to protect itself.* When collective nouns are used in sentences that refer to individual members of the group, plural verb forms and pronouns can be used. *The herd were wandering off in all different directions.*

Note that special subject-verb agreement problems are posed by sentences that use collective nouns as subjects:

Faulty Agreement: Collective Noun-Verb
Nothing are, the batch are done, the group decide

Correct Agreement: Collective Noun-Verb
The committee thinks, the herd stampedes, all members of the group decide

See also **AMOUNTS.**

Colloquial language

Colloquial language consists of casual or informal words and constructions that are appropriate in familiar speech and in some kinds of journalism, but are considered lax in serious, formal discourse. Colloquial words include **TV** for **television, guy** or **gal** for **man** or **woman, cruise** for **succeed easily,** and **choke** for **fail disgracefully.**

See also NONSTANDARD USAGE.

Colons

Colons are most commonly used after independent clauses to introduce additional information about a subject the clause has already raised. *I have three piranhas: Sleepy, Dimples, and Fang. Several people, on learning I have piranhas, have asked the same question: "How many fingers do you have?"*

Colons should be used to introduce additional information only after an independent clause. The following sentence misuses the colon by inserting it in the middle of an independent clause: *The most notable quality of piranhas is: hunger.*

Colons have a variety of additional uses. They are used after the salutation in a business letter: *Dear Sir or Madam:* They are used to separate titles from subtitles: *Piranhas as Pets: Putting the Care in Care and Feeding.* They are also used for separating hours from minutes when telling the time: **4:30.**

Combining forms

Combining forms are elements that can be combined with words and other elements to form new words. They may be prefixes or suffixes.

See also **PREFIXES** and **SUFFIXES**.

Commands

Commands are imperative sentences. They may consist of the verb alone, since the subject (you) is implied, and these sentences often conclude with exclamation points. *Walk!*

Commas

In general, commas are used to make written sentences easier to understand. They belong before coordinating the conjunctions **and, but, for, or, so,** and **yet** when these words are used to join independent clauses. *I know something about your girlfriend that you don't know, but I'm not going to tell you what it is.*

Commas should also be used after words and phrases that precede or introduce the main clause. *Incidentally, lots of other people know, too. With so many people talking about it, you're bound to find out eventually.*

Commas may set off inessential information that occurs in the middle of a main clause. *Her friend Karen, who hates keeping secrets, told me all about it.*

Commas may also emphasize contrasts. *She did something that made her glad, not sorry.*

Commas are also used to separate elements in a series of three or more. *Karen also told Jim, Abdul, Gloria, and Kim.*

Commas should not be used to set off information

that is necessary for the main clause to make sense. *Everyone who works the morning shift must have found out by now.*

Commas should be used to separate adjectives that modify the same noun. *I heard she had on a tight, slinky dress.* However, commas should not be used to separate adjectives that modify the same noun unequally. *She also had bright red lipstick on.*

See also DASHES and SEMICOLONS.

Comma splices

Comma splices are grammatical errors caused by joining two sentences with a comma rather than separating them with a period. Comma splices are also called fused sentences. *I'm tired, I wish I were home in bed.* Here the two clauses should be written as distinct sentences separated by a period. *I'm tired. I wish I were home in bed.*

common, mutual, shared

Common, mutual, and **shared** have similar meanings, but **mutual** is generally used to refer to feelings that are shared between two people. Friends and acquaintances may also be mutual. *She and I have a mutual dislike for our mutual acquaintance.* **Common** differs from **shared** in that **common** connotes significant, identifying features. *We have our spiritual values in common. We share our susceptibility to sunburn.* **Common** may also refer to things shared by any number; **mutual,** however, refers to things shared between two.

Common nouns

Common nouns, as opposed to proper names, are nouns that refer to things that are considered identical to others of their kind. Proper names, on the other hand, refer to individual, one-of-a kind people, places, and things.

Comparative form

Comparative form is the form taken by adjectives and adverbs that compare like nouns according to the degree to which they possess the qualities they describe. *Your right eye is greener than your left. Does it see more clearly?* Here **greener** is a comparative adjective and **more clearly** is a comparative adverb. Contrast comparative form with the superlative and positive forms.

See also ADJECTIVES; ADVERBS; COMPARISON; POS-ITIVE FORM; and SUPERLATIVE FORM.

compared to, compared with

Compare is a transitive verb that takes the preposition, **to. Compared with** is incorrect. *Compared to other athletes, Susan is rather small.*

Comparison

Adverbs and adjectives indicate different degrees of comparison by their forms. These forms may be positive, comparative, or superlative. Positive forms simply modify without comparing: **the big dog.** Comparative forms show a comparison of two things: **the bigger dog.** Superlative forms indicate extremes: **the biggest dog.**

Superlative form should not be used to compare two things only. It is thus incorrect to say, *The sedan gets the best gas mileage of the two cars.* It is more accurate to say, *The sedan gets the better gas mileage of the two cars.*

Double comparisons are redundant and unacceptable. *The house looks more bigger from the north side.*

Incomplete comparisons are also unacceptable in formal writing. When comparisons are made, the sentence that makes them should indicate both terms being compared. It is incorrect to say *Spending time in Mexico was better than at home.* Here **spending time** cannot be compared to **at home.** The sentence should read *Spending time in Mexico was better than spending it at home.* Many incomplete comparisons occur in sentences that use the word **than,** as in the example above. Incomplete comparisons also result from using **such** or **so** as terms of emphasis rather than as terms of comparison. *You are so lucky. You have such good luck.* Incomplete comparisons are also a familiar advertising technique. Many ads use comparative terms such as **more** and **bigger** without presenting two terms for comparison. *You get more out of our product.*

Incomplete Comparisons
Dogs can be such a nuisance. Late-night barking is so annoying. Playing soccer in your neighborhood is more fun than mine. Save more now! Eat less faster!

See also SO; SUCH; and THAN, THEN.

complacent, complaisant
A **complacent** person is pleasing to him- or herself. **Complacence** also suggests an unwillingness to change or adjust to the wishes of others. A **complaisant** person is pleasing to others.

Complement

A complement is an adjective or noun that is neither the subject nor the object in a sentence containing a linking verb. A complement may be a subject complement or an object complement. A subject complement appears after a linking verb and modifies the subject of the sentence. It is that which is joined by the linking verb to the subject. *The garlic butter became rancid.* Here **rancid** is the complement of the subject, **garlic butter.**

An object complement also appears in sentences with linking verbs, but it modifies the object, rather than the subject, of the sentence. *The other square dancers knocked me silly.* Here **silly** is the complement of the object, **me.**

See also CASE; OBJECTS; and SUBJECT.

complement, compliment

Complement means to complete or make whole. *Catsup complements any meal consisting of deep-fried foods.* **Compliment** means to make an approving remark. *I must compliment you on your taste in condiments.*

complete, replete

Complete means whole or finished. *I have a complete set of Nehi bottle caps.* **Replete** means **full** or **having in abundance** and takes the preposition **with.** *My bottle cap collection is replete with caps made in the 1950s.*

Complex sentence

A complex sentence contains at least two clauses, one of which is independent and one of which is dependent. *If I can't shuffle my feet, I'll fall over.*

See also COMPOUND SENTENCE; COMPOUND-COMPLEX SENTENCE; and SIMPLE SENTENCES.

Compound adjective

A compound adjective is formed when two or more words are used together to modify the same noun. A hyphen (-) should be used to indicate that the two words form a single modifier if the modifier comes before the noun it modifies. *This is a user-friendly computer.* If the compound adjective does not occur directly before the noun it modifies, a hyphen is unnecessary. *This conputer is user friendly.*

Compound-complex sentence

A compound-complex sentence is made up of two or more independent clauses and at least one dependent clause.

Although I can't understand a word you say, I'm glad you talk a lot, since you have a nice voice. Care should be taken in writing compound-complex sentences to avoid excessive coordination and comma splices.

See also COMMA SPLICES and EXCESSIVE COORDINATION.

Compound construction

A compound construction consists of two or more words or groups of words that function in the same way. It may take the form of a compound noun, a compound adjective, a compound subject, a compound predicate, or a compound sentence. *Aesop was a storyteller.* Here **storyteller** is a compound noun. *The human-animal characters in his beast fables are familiar to all.* Here **human-animal** is a compound adjective. *The grasshopper and the ant disagree.* Here **the grasshopper and the ant** is a compound subject. *The grasshopper eats and sleeps.* Here **eats and sleeps** is a compound predicate. *The grasshopper is lazy, but the ant works hard.* This sentence is a compound sentence.

See also COMPOUND NOUN; COMPOUND SENTENCE; and COMPOUND SUBJECT.

Compound noun

Compound nouns are nouns made up of two or more words such as *Adam's apple, boot camp,* and *belly button.*

See also COMPOUND CONSTRUCTION.

Compound sentence

A compound sentence consists of two independent clauses. *I took one little sip and she nearly throttled me.*

See also COMPOUND CONSTRUCTION.

Compound subject

A compound subject consists of two nouns. *My mother and your brother think we're in church.*

See also COMPOUND CONSTRUCTION.

comprehend, apprehend

See also APPREHEND, COMPREHEND.

compulsory, mandatory

Compulsory and **mandatory** both mean **required** but **compulsory** bears the additional sense, **enforced.** Thus wearing seat belts is mandatory whereas stopping at red lights is compulsory.

Conciseness

Conciseness is the desirable quality of discourse not padded with unnecessary words. Conciseness differs from brevity in that a concise discussion can be long and include details and explanations yet still move efficiently from point to point.

Verbs supply an especially useful measure of concise writing. Direct, accurate verbs in the active voice move prose forward more efficiently than passive constructions, expletive constructions, and other often unnecessary phrases based on the weak verb, **be,** including its forms, **is, was, are, am,** etc.

Too many **be** formations often result when writing tries to *explain* what it *should* be doing rather than *doing* what it should do. Phrases like *it can be shown that . . .* and *this is evident when we realize . . .* simply describe the process of understanding—a process that takes place more easily without such empty gestures.

A major barrier to conciseness is lack of experience with and confidence in the language. Writers who are uncertain as to whether their words actually convey their meaning tend to repeat themselves unnecessarily and to use a number of superfluous words in the hope that some of them will get their message across. The best way to avoid this problem is to weigh one's writing word by word, sentence by sentence, and paragraph by paragraph.

Concrete language

Concrete language refers to things that can be perceived by one or more of the five senses. Concrete language is useful in clarifying abstract and general discussion. Abstract and general language is useful in showing the significance of concrete language. *The smell of rotten lemons was interesting and not entirely unpleasant.* Here **rotten lemons** is the only concrete term in the sentence. It adds specificity to the general term, **smell.** The abstract terms, **interesting** and **not unpleasant,** explain the significance of the general and concrete terms.

See also **ABSTRACT LANGUAGE** and **GENERAL TERMS.**

Conditional sentences

Conditional sentences concern situations whose truth depends on circumstances that may or may not actually exist. They are almost always complex sentences, consisting of a dependent clause stating a condition and an independent clause stating what is, was, will be, or would be true given the condition. *If you eat all your jellyfish, you can have some candied ants for dessert.*

There are three kinds of conditional sentences: factual, predictive, and speculative. In conditional sentences that are factual, the verb tense in the dependent and independent clauses may be either past or present, but it must agree in both. *Every time I eat candied ants, their legs get stuck between my teeth. When I last ate candied ants, I thought of the American Revolution.*

Predictive conditional sentences concern events that might happen in the future. In such sentences, the dependent clause should take the present tense and the independent clause should take the future tense. *If I have candied ants for lunch tomorrow, I'll give you some.*

Speculative conditional sentences concern situations that are not true, but would be true under the circumstances they describe. In such sentences, the independent clause takes the present tense combined with **could, might,** or **would,** while the dependent clause takes a special form of the past tense known as the subjunctive mood. The subjunctive mood indicates that the action of the verb did not actually take place. *If he were not so finicky, he would try some of my candied ants.*

The subjunctive mood presents a special source of difficulty for many because not all verbs have a distinct subjunctive form and, even for those that do, it is used only with certain pronouns, **I, he, she,** and **it,** and with singular nouns. Because speculative conditional sentences always use the past tense form of the verb, **to be,** they require the subjunctive mood whenever **I, he, she,** or **it** is the subject.

Faulty Subjunctive
*If I **was** wealthy; even if you **have** time; †if he sun be shining now*

Correct Subjunctive
*If I **had** the money; if such **be** your preference; if he **were** shorter*

See also CLAUSE and MOOD OF VERB.

confute, refute

Refute means to supply evidence against a claim or theory. *These sunflower seed shells all over the living room refute your theory that George is a considerate house* *guest.* **Confute** means not only to supply evidence against, but to wholly disprove. Thus **refute** is milder than **confute.** Milder still is **rebut.**

See also **REBUT, REFUTE.**

Conjugation
See also **VERB CONJUGATION.**

Conjunctions
Conjunctions join parts of a sentence in one of three logical relationships: coordinating, correlative, and subordinating. Coordinating conjunctions are **and, but, for, nor, or, so,** and **yet.** They join words and phrases that have equivalent functions. *You are not especially good looking, nor are you intelligent.* Here the conjunction **nor** joins two independent clauses.

Correlative conjunctions, like coordinating conjunctions, join equivalent words and phrases, but, unlike coordinating conjunctions, they require two words to do so. Correlative conjunctions are **as . . . as, both . . . and, either . . . or, neither . . . nor, not . . . but,** and **whether . . . or.** *As soon as you are through, start again.* Here, **soon** and **as you are through** are adverbs that modify the verb, **start.**

Subordinating conjunctions turn independent clauses into dependent clauses and join them in a logical relationship with a different independent clause. Subordinating conjunctions are **after, although, as, because, before, even, if, once, since, though, unless, until, when,** and **while.** *Honk if you are tired of noise pollution.* Here the subordinating conjunction, **if,** turns the clause, **you are tired of noise pollution** into a dependent clause and relates it to the independent clause, **honk.**

Conjunctive adverbs

Conjunctive adverbs join two independent clauses in a logical relationship within a single sentence. Similarly, they establish a logical relationship between two sentences. Some conjunctive adverbs are **also, anyway, besides, consequently, finally, hence, incidentally, meanwhile, moreover, nevertheless, similarly,** and **therefore.** *The air pressure dropped and, consequently, it rained.*

Connecting words

See also CONJUNCTIONS.

Connotation

The connotation of a word is a secondary meaning it may have acquired through association. For example, because people often associate nature with health, the word **natural** has a positive connotation.

conscience, conscious

Conscience refers to the ability to distinguish between right and wrong. It is used most often as a noun. **Conscious** is an adjective meaning **aware.**

consider

Consider may be used either as a transitive or intransitive verb meaning **judge.** Used without a preposition or with **to be,** it refers to a general assessment of a person, thing, or situation. *I consider you to be among the most eminent of bottle cap collectors.* Here **to be** may be omitted or included. Together with the preposition **as,** consider refers to a specific capacity. *Bottle caps are of tremendous importance when we consider them as cultural artifacts.*

Consider should not be used as a synonym for **esteem.** Thus it is inaccurate to say, *I consider you as a friend.* This statement should read, *I esteem you as a friend,* or *I consider you to be a friend,* or, *I consider you as a friend and find you satisfactory.*

See also AS, LIKE.

considerable, considerably

Considerable is an adjective used in regard to factors that should be taken into account. It is used informally as an intensifier, but should not be so used in formal writing. *She has a considerable backhand.* This sentence makes inappropriate use of **considerable,** which should be used to describe how things relate to an argument or line of reasoning. *Her backhand is considerable as evidence of her flexibility.* **Considerably** should be avoided altogether in formal discourse, since it serves no other purpose than intensification.

consist of, consist in

Consist of means **be made up of.** *Cola consists of water, sugar, and chemicals.* **Consist in** means **include.** It is often used figuratively to refer to abstract terms to mean **is defined (in whole or in part) by.** *Evil consists in ignorance as well as in selfishness.*

See also ABSTRACT LANGUAGE and FIGURATIVE LANGUAGE.

Consistency

Consistency is a desirable quality of writing and speech that is achieved by using words in accordance with their standard acceptation and by avoiding unnecessary shifts between plural and singular pronouns, among first, second, and third person pronouns, shifts in verb tense, and shifts between direct and indirect discourse.

When a subject is introduced as either plural or singular, any pronoun that refers to the subject should be consistent in number. This rule applies within a single sentence as well as when proceeding from one sentence to the next. *When you use a coat as a gunny sack it is likely to get wet or dirty. They are best used to serve the purpose for which they were made.* Here there is an unwarranted shift from the singular noun, **coat** to the plural pronoun, **they.**

Shifts among first, second, and third person pronouns should also be avoided. *When one is hungry, you do things that others would not.* Here there is an unnecessary shift from the third person pronoun, **one,** to the second person pronoun, **you.**

Inappropriate shifts in verb tense should also be avoided. *I'm standing there minding my own business and I got splashed by a car.* Here the shift from the present tense verb, **am standing,** to the past tense verb, **got splashed,** is unnecessary.

Sometimes it is necessary to shift verb tenses, as when a single sentence refers to different periods of time. *We wore purple at the wedding but we're going naked to the reception.*

See also **AGREEMENT.**

consul, council, counsel
Consul is a specific term meaning **foreign service officer.** A council is a group that meets to deliberate problems concerning a larger body or organization. A counsel is an adviser. **Counsel** may also be used as a noun meaning **advice.**

contemporary, contemporaneous
Contemporary is an adjective that may be used to refer to any period of time that is the context of discussion. It should not be used, therefore, as a synonym for **modern** in a discussion of past events. The following statement is ambiguous and should be made more clear: *The author of the medieval poem, "Piers Plowman," did not have access to contemporary farming technology.* In this case, **contemporaneous** may be substituted for **contemporary** to avoid ambiguity.

contemptible, contemptuous
Contemptible is an adjective meaning **worthy of contempt.** *The pleasure they take in the sufferings of others is contemptible.* **Contemptuous** is an adjective describing the attitude of those who despise things or people. *She had a contemptuous expression on her face when I arrived an hour late.*

Context
Context is the frame or background necessary for presenting ideas in written form. Establishing a context for one's own written work involves relating it to other relevant ideas and assumptions. These ideas and assumptions must be attributed to recognizable sources.

A piece of persuasive writing does not simply convey truth but shows how its assertions relate to other similar and/or contrary ideas. Thus context enables a writer to demonstrate the relevance and significance of his or her work by showing what others do not already know or by showing that what others think is of limited value.

See also **ATTRIBUTION** and **ORIGINALITY**.

continual, continuous

Continual and **continuous** both mean **ongoing** but **continual** refers to the intermittent repetition of events. *The hitchhiker made continual observations about the weather.* **Continuous** refers to uninterrupted action. *I was tired after six hours of continuous driving.*

Contractions

Contractions are words made by combining and sometimes shortening other words, using an apostrophe to indicate where a letter or letters have been taken out. **Don't** is a contraction for **do not, it's** is a contraction for **it is.** Contractions are acceptable in informal writing but should be avoided in formal writing.

convince

Convince, unlike its synonym, **persuade,** should not be used with the preposition **to.** Thus it is inappropriate to say, *I convinced her to change her mind.* One may say instead, *I convinced her that she should change her mind,* or *I convinced her of following my plan.*

Coordination

Coordination is the bringing together of two words or word groups that have equal importance. *I thought you might not be home, but I rang the bell anyway.* In this sentence, the coordinating conjunction, **but,** joins two independent clauses.

Faulty coordination is a failure to relate two words or word groups with an appropriate logical connection. *I thought you might not be home, but the weather is nice today.* Here the logical relationship suggested by the coordinating conjunction, **but,** misrepresents the actual relationship between the ideas in the two clauses, which should be separated into different sentences.

Correlative conjunctions

Correlative conjunctions are paired conjunctions such as **as . . . as, either . . . or, not . . . but,** and **whether . . . or** that connect and relate equivalent words and word groups.

See also CONJUNCTIONS.

could have, of

Because **have** and **of** are often pronounced similarly when spoken, the two words are often confused when written. Only **have** should be used after helping verbs such as **could, would,** and **may.** *We could have finished an hour earlier.*

council, counsel, consul

See also CONSUL, COUNCIL, COUNSEL.

Count nouns

Count nouns, as opposed to mass nouns and collective nouns, refer to specific things that can be counted. When singular, they should be preceded by **a, an,** or **the.** *The flowers bloomed early.*

See also AMOUNT, NUMBER; COLLECTIVE NOUNS; and MASS NOUNS.

couple

Couple is a collective noun that may take either a plural or a singular verb. When used to refer to a number of things, the preposition, **of,** should be used. *We had a couple of drinks.*

See also COLLECTIVE NOUNS.

credence, credibility, credulity

Credence means **trust** or **belief.** *We could not give credence to his improbable story.* **Credibility** means **able to induce belief.** *Her credibility, based on years of experience in the field, was unassailable.* **Credulity** means **gullibility** or **tendency to believe.** *His credulity made him an easy target for hustlers.*

crisis, crises

The plural form of **crisis** is not **crisises,** but **crises.** The plural of many nouns ending -**is** is formed in a similar way: **theses, analyses, oases.**

criteria, criterion

Criteria is the plural form of the singular noun, **criterion.**

D

Dangling modifiers

A dangling modifier is an adjective or adverb clause that does not refer to the subject or predicate of the sentence to which it belongs and is therefore improper. *Nearly out of gas, the road seemed endless.* This sentence says that the road was nearly out of gas, which is logically impossible. The modifier, **nearly out of gas,** is dangling because it has no logical referent.

Dangling modifiers, which are incorrect forms, should not be confused with absolute phrases, which are acceptable. *The car having run low on gas, the road seemed endless.*

Dangling Modifiers
Up to her ears in debt, the dog ate her bankroll. Bored with the movie, even the popcorn seemed bland. Muscles aching, the finish line seemed miles away.

See also **ABSOLUTE PHRASES** and **MODIFIERS.**

Dashes

Dashes—may be used to signal an interruption of a standard grammatical sentence or in place of commas, colons, or parentheses when a phrase or series might otherwise seem confusing. Of all punctuation marks, dashes supply the most emphatic means of separating segments of a sentence. *Of the many kinds of dogs at the show—collies, dachshunds, poodles, labs, and terriers—the Saint Bernards drool the most. Their saliva—no! not on my coat!—is especially thick and sticky.*

Dashes are used informally more frequently than in formal writing. Note that there is no separation between a dash and its adjacent words. A dash may be formed on a typewriter by joining two hyphens.

dastardly
Dastardly is sometimes used loosely to refer to anyone who does bad things and to the things they do. More specifically, however, it should be used to refer to cowardly people and acts. *Blaming your underlings for your mistakes is a dastardly practice.*

data, datum
Data is the plural form of the singular noun, **datum.**

deadly, deathly
Deadly may be used to refer to things that cause death. *Many deadly mushrooms resemble edible ones.* **Deathly** may be used to refer to things that suggest death. *His face turned a deathly color.*

debut
Debut is properly a noun and should not be used as a verb. Use of **debut** as a transitive verb is especially inappropriate in formal writing. *I will debut my new hairstyle tomorrow.*

decisive, incisive

Decisive is an adjective or adverb meaning **with assurance** or **determining.** *The rap of the judge's gavel is always a decisive gesture.* **Incisive** is used in reference to ideas and means **penetrating.** *No one tried to refute her incisive observation.*

Declarative mood

The declarative mood, also known as the indicative mood, is one of three verb moods along with the subjunctive and imperative moods. Verb mood shows that the action of the verb is factual, is a command, or is subject to doubt. The declarative mood, the most common of the three, is used for factual assertions. *Reality is distracting.*

Declension

Declension refers to the various case forms of nouns and pronouns. **Declension** is more commonly used in the context of Latin grammar than in English since case is more important in Latin.

See also CASE.

decry, descry

Decry means **denounce.** *Only the neurotic and the hypocritical decry all material values.* **Descry** means **see** or **recognize.** *I descried my cousin at the other end of the bowling alley.*

defective, deficient

Defective means **flawed.** *This sandal is defective; the strap is broken.* **Deficient** means **lacking in quality or**

amount, but is most often used in reference to quantity. *The shoe salesman was deficient in brains; he kept trying to put the left shoe on my right foot.*

definite, definitive

Definite means **certain** or **clear.** It is generally used to refer to matters of fact. *We have definite plans to go fishing.* **Definitive** means **conclusive** and is most often used in regard to matters of interpretation. *I am working on a definitive study of prewar bottle caps.*

Definite article

The definite article, **the,** shows that the word or words following it refer to a particular thing or things.

See also A, AN, THE and ARTICLES.

deliberate, deliberative

As an adjective, **deliberate** means **intentional.** *The food fight was a deliberate means of getting attention.* As a verb, **deliberate** means **consider.** *I had to deliberate before buying the rug.* **Deliberative** is an adjective that suggests intention but also uncertainty. It refers to the patient mulling over possibilities. *His deliberative bargaining technique often made merchants give him a good price out of sheer impatience.*

delusion, illusion

Both **delusion** and **illusion** mean **imaginary appearance,** but **delusion** also suggests mistaken belief. *He suffers from the delusion of having a good singing voice.* **Illusion** usually refers to an artificial representation that may or may not be believed. *The architecture created the illusion of spaciousness.*

Demonstrative pronouns

Demonstrative pronouns are one of five classes of pronouns that refer to nouns in different ways. Other kinds of pronouns are personal, relative, indefinite, and interrogative. Demonstrative pronouns include **this, that these,** and **those** and refer to specific things that are usually mentioned in or near the sentence in which the pronoun appears. They are often used to introduce things that may subsequently be referred to with the personal pronoun, **it** or **they.** *If these anteaters could open their mouths wider, they would look like furry crocodiles.* Here **these** is a demonstrative pronoun and **they** is a personal pronoun.

Demonstrative pronouns should not be inflected to show possession. It is incorrect to say *This doohickey is those's.* This sentence should read, *This doohickey is one of those.*

See also **PRONOUNS.**

Denotation

As opposed to connotation, denotation is the literal meaning of a word or words, uncolored by emotional association. The denotation of the word **carrion** is edible meat that has not been killed and prepared for the eater.

depend

In formal writing, **depend** should always be followed by the preposition **on,** or **upon. Thus** it is inappropriate to say, **it depends who, it depends how, it depends whether** or **it depends when.**

Dependent clauses

Also called subordinate clauses, dependent clauses resemble independent or main clauses in that they contain both a subject and a verb, but they differ in that they cannot form complete sentences on their own without additional information. They begin with words that indicate their subordination such as **after, although, as, because, before, if, since, though, unless, until, what, when, whether,** and **while.** They can be used as adjectives or as adverbs. *The grain of pollen that made me sneeze lodged firmly into a tiny dent in my mucous membrane, while I secreted a copious amount of fluid.* Here the dependent clause, **that made me sneeze,** serves as an adjective modifying the subject, **grain of pollen,** while the dependent clause, **while I secreted a copious amount of fluid,** serves as an adverb modifying the verb, **lodged.**

deprecate, depreciate

Deprecate means **speak badly of.** *The political parties continually deprecate one another.* **Depreciate** means **belittle** or **make less valuable.** *Multiculturalists depreciate a narrow conception of progress.*

descry, decry

See also DECRY, DESCRY.

Determiners

Determiners are used to indicate the presence of a noun. They include the articles **a, an,** and **the** and the possessive personal pronouns, **my** and **your.**

See also A, AN, THE and PRONOUNS.

device, devise

Device is a noun meaning **invention**. **Devise** is the verb form of the noun, **device**, meaning **to invent**.

diagnosis, prognosis

A diagnosis is the identification of a disease or diseases. *A thorough diagnosis failed to reveal the tumor.* A prognosis is the prediction of the outcome or course of a disease. *Someone who is generally in good shape should receive a more favorable prognosis for an illness than someone who isn't.* **Prognosis** is sometimes used more broadly and colloquially to mean **prediction.** *The weatherman's prognosis is not good.*

Dialects

Dialects are variants of a language. Generally, different dialects of the same language are mutually understandable in spite of differences in vocabulary, syntax, and pronunciation.

See also **BLACK ENGLISH.**

Diction

Diction refers to word choice. It can be formal or casual. Formal diction is appropriate for subjects that are serious and/or complicated and therefore require clear, precise expression.

See also **INFLATED DICTION.**

die

Die takes the preposition **of,** not **from.** It is incorrect to say, *He died from cancer.*

different from, different than
Different from is generally more acceptable than **different than**. *Your carrots are different from mine.*

dilemma, quandary
Dilemma should be used to refer to the difficulty in deciding between two options, not among three or more. Thus it is inappropriate to say, *All of the possibilities posed a dilemma.* A more accurate term here is **quandary**.

Direct address
Direct address is a way of speaking or writing in which the person or persons being addressed are explicitly identified. *Fathers, be good to your children. When you finish washing the car you may mow the lawn.* Contrast indirect address: *Fathers should be good to their children. Those who have finished washing the car may mow the lawn.*

Direct object
The direct object is the part of speech that receives the action of the verb. *The snake ate the frog.* Here, **frog** is the direct object of the verb, **ate.** Unlike indirect objects, direct objects do not take prepositions such as **to, for, with, at,** and **by.**

discomfit, discomfort
Traditionally, **discomfit** was used only to mean **defeat** or **foil.** It is properly used today to mean **embarrass.** Recently, it has become synonymous with **discomfort,** its casual usage.

Discourse

Discourse is verbal communication in speech or writing. Grammatically speaking, it may be direct or indirect.

See also DISCOURSE, LANGUAGE, and INDIRECT DISCOURSE.

discourse, language

Discourse and **language** both refer to writing as well as speech. **Discourse,** unlike **language,** implies that writing and speech are organized along social, political, and/or economic lines. Thus discourse does not simply contain meaning but determines the way the effect of meaning is produced and maintained in the service of one or more social agendas or ideologies.

See also IDEOLOGY, KNOWLEDGE and SELF, SUBJECTIVITY.

disinterested, uninterested

Disinterested means impartial, not having any stake in an outcome. It should not be confused with **uninterested,** which means bored, not inclined to pay attention.

discreet, discrete

Discreet means **tactful.** *My ex-brother-in-law greeted me with a discreet nod when he saw me with Denise.* **Discrete** means **separate** or **individual.** *We were too far away to see the zebras as discrete entities.*

distinct, distinctive

Distinct means **clearly recognizable.** *Skunks have a distinct odor.* **Distinctive** means **unusual,** or **pertaining**

solely to an individual. *If you look closely, you can see that her nose has a distinctive shape.*

dived, dove

Either **dived** or **dove** may be used as the past tense of the verb, **dive. Dived,** however, is generally preferred. **Dived** should also be used as the past participle of **dive.**

done

Done should not be used to mean **finished** when it might be taken to mean **in process.** The following sentence is ambiguous: *The project will be done next month.*

don't, doesn't

In standard English, **don't** is the proper form of the verb to use with **I, you, we,** and **they. Doesn't** is used with **he, she,** and **it.** Some dialects of English, including Black English, use **don't** instead of **doesn't.** From the standpoint of standard English, this is considered improper.

See also **BLACK ENGLISH.**

Double comparisons

Double comparisons, such as **more better** and **most hardest,** are redundant and considered incorrect in standard English.

Double negatives

Double negatives usually involve using **not** and **no** in the same sentence. *There haven't been no good operas at the Met all season.* Many double negatives are redundant and considered incorrect in standard English. Some double negatives are acceptable, as when one negative negates the other, resulting in a positive assertion. *They are not always unpredictable.* In general, however, double negatives should be avoided, since positive assertions are clearer and more direct.

doubtless, no doubt, undoubtedly

Doubtless and **no doubt** provide extremely weak emphasis, suggesting speculation or concession as much as certainty. *No doubt you are right, but it is not very important.* **Undoubtedly** provides a strong emphasis, suggesting conviction. *Undoubtedly you are right and you are sure to convince others.*

See also EMPHASIS.

dozen, dozens

Dozen is used to refer specific numbers that are multiples of twelve. *We scrambled four dozen eggs.* **Dozens** is used to refer to an estimated amount of thirty or more. *We scrambled dozens of eggs.*

drink, drunk

Drunk is properly used as the past participle of **drink.** *I have drunk all I want.* **Drank,** the standard past tense form, is nonstandard as the past participle, as is **drunken.**

See also PARTICIPLES.

drown

The past tense and past participle form of **drown** is **drowned. Drownded** is nonstandard.

due to

Due to is properly used together with a linking verb. *His shyness was due to a speech impediment.* **Due to** should not be used unless that which is due is stated in noun form. Thus it is incorrect to say, *He was shy due to a speech impediment.*

dying, dyeing

Dying is the gerund form of the verb, **die,** meaning **cease to live. Dyeing** is the gerund form of the verb **dye,** which means **stain with a colored liquid.**

E

each
Each is an indefinite pronoun that refers to a singular thing. It therefore requires a singular verb. *Each of the animals is housebroken.*

eager, anxious
Eager and **anxious** are both adjectives. **Anxious** is often misused to mean **eager**. **Eager** means extremely willing and takes the preposition, **to**. **Anxious** means worried and takes the proposition, **about**. Hence, it is incorrect to say, *We are anxious to start the meeting.* One should say, *We are eager to start the meeting,* or, *We are anxious about starting the meeting.*

effect, affect
See also **AFFECT, EFFECT.**

e.g., i.e.
E.g. and **i.e.** are Latin abbreviations. **E.g.** stands for *exempli gratia* and means **for example.** *Ice cream now comes with a lot of disgusting stuff inside, e.g., raw cookie dough.* **E.g.** is sometimes confused with **i.e.** which stands for **id est** and means **that is.** **I.e.** should be used to introduce, not an example, but a definition. *One particularly nauseating variety of ice cream is Mr.*

McGoo, i.e., pistachio ice cream with marshmallow, caramel, and salt water taffy.

egoist, egotist
An **egoist** is a selfish person. An **egotist** is a boastful person.

either, or
Either . . . or is a paired correlative conjunction used to indicate that two terms are applicable. When the terms are singular, they should take a singular verb form. *Either Heide or Tina is eating out today.* When the terms are plural, they should take a plural verb form. *Either the Smiths or the Hoovers were wrong on the issue.* However, if one term is singular and the other plural, the verb agrees with the subject closest to it. *Either Emily or the Vanderbuilts are joining us tonight.* **Either** should never be linked with **nor** which belongs with **neither**.

See also NEITHER, NOR.

elder, older
Elder and **older** both mean **of greater age,** but **elder** refers exclusively to people.

elicit, illicit
Elicit is a verb meaning **produce by drawing out,** said of reactions. **Illicit** is an adjective meaning **not allowed.** *Your illicit behavior will elicit a harsh response by the authorities.*

Ellipsis

An ellipsis is a punctuation mark made with three dots (. . .) and is properly used to indicate omissions from a quotation. *"Canon to the left of them, . . . to the right of them."*

Ellipses may also be used to indicate a logical omission or an omitted conclusion. *And in the end, we realized . . .* This last usage should be restricted to creative writing and is inappropriate in formal discourse.

elude, allude

Elude means **avoid capture or pursuit.** *The gazelles that elude the tigers must contend with parasites.* **Elude** may also be used in reference to ideas to mean **escape comprehension.** *The explanation for your behavior eludes me.* **Allude** means **refer indirectly.** *In humming "Yankee Doodle" we allude to your hat.*

Embedded clauses

Embedded clauses are clauses that are inserted into the middle of other clauses. They are grammatically acceptable when set off by commas or other parenthetical marks such as dashes or parentheses. *Tuna fish, because it is convenient and inexpensive, is a popular lunch food.* Here, **because it is convenient and inexpensive** is an embedded clause inserted in the middle of the main clause.

See also CLAUSES; COMMAS; and PARENTHESES.

eminent, immanent, imminent

Eminent means **great** or **illustrious** and is used to refer to people. *Aren't you the eminent bottle cap collector?*

Immanent means **inward** or **subjective.** *Her religion is more immanent than doctrinal.* **Imminent** means **about to happen.** *She knew as she was eating that heartburn was imminent.*

emote
Emote is a nonstandard back-formation that should be avoided in formal writing.

See also **BACK-FORMATION.**

empathy, sympathy
Empathy is a more specific term than **sympathy,** indicating an identification with another based on shared feelings. *Our empathy does not extend beyond a mutual dislike of soap operas.* **Sympathy** is the feeling of concern for another's pain. *Many who request loans get only sympathy.*

Emphasis
Ideas may be emphasized in a variety of ways, including by underlining and italicizing words, adding an exclamation mark (!) to the end of a sentence, by means of dashes (—) to set off important phrases, and by using words and phrases like **above all, indeed,** and **in fact.** In addition, emphasis can be indicated by subordinating related ideas to those that are more important with subordinating conjunctions such as **after, although, because, since,** and **until.**

See also **DASHES; ITALICS; SUBORDINATION;** and **UNDERLINE.**

End punctuation

End punctuation consists of marks that indicate the end of a sentence. These include periods **(.)**, question marks **(?)**, and exclamation marks **(!)**. Less commonly, ellipses may serve as end punctuation. Dashes are sometimes used informally as end punctuation.

end result

The phrase, **end result,** is redundant and should be avoided.

See also **REDUNDANCY.**

enhance, augment

See also **AUGMENT, ENHANCE.**

enormity, enormous

Enormity should not be used to refer to things of great size unless they are also morally reprehensible. Thus it is incorrect to say, *The children were delighted by the elephant's enormity.* **Enormity** should be used only to refer to things that are morally outrageous. *The enormity of your crimes makes them unforgivable.* **Enormous,** however, may be used in reference to size alone. *The elephant was enormous.*

ensure, assure, insure

See also **ASSURE, ENSURE, INSURE.**

enthused

Enthused is a nonstandard back-formation of the adjective, **enthusiastic. Enthusiastic** is more acceptable in formal writing.

See also **BACK-FORMATION.**

entomologist, etymologist

An **entomologist** studies insects. An **etymologist** studies word origins and derivations.

epithet

Epithet is often used to mean **derogatory phrase,** but may be used to mean any descriptive phrase. *We gave him the epithet, 'Doer of Good Deeds'.*

equal, more

Equal is an absolute adjective that should not be used with comparative terms such as **more** except when an ironic effect is desired. *Some people are more equal than others.*

See also **ABSOLUTE TERMS.**

errata

Errata is a plural term and should be used with plural verbs and pronouns. *These errata have been corrected.* The singular form of **errata** is **erratum.**

escape

Escape should be used with the preposition, **from.** *We escaped from the boring lecture.* It is incorrect not to use from in such cases.

esoteric, exoteric

Both **esoteric** and **exoteric** refer to ideas. Esoteric ideas are those shared by a small, specialized group; hence they are unfamiliar to most people. *The study of ancient philosophy is becoming increasingly esoteric.* **Exoteric** means **generally known.** *The rules of baseball are becoming increasingly exoteric all over the world.*

Essential clauses and phrases

Essential or necessary clauses and phrases are word groups that are semantically though not structurally necessary to the sentences to which they belong. Unlike inessential clauses and phrases, they contain information that completes an idea presented by the main clause. *All buildings over four stories tall should have elevators.* The phrase **over four stories tall** is necessary since without it, the meaning of the sentence would be contradicted. Essential clauses and phrases should not be separated from the rest of the sentence with commas.

See also NONESSENTIAL CLAUSES AND PHRASES.

etc.

Etc. is an abbreviation for the Latin phrase, *et cetera,* meaning **and other things.** It may be used to indicate that a list is partial rather than complete, but its use is redundant after lists that are introduced with **including, such as, for example,** etc., since these terms indicate that the following examples do not exhaust all possibilities.

See also ABBREVIATIONS and REDUNDANCY.

Euphemisms

Euphemisms are terms that are used in place of harsh words that might be considered painful or offensive. Some euphemisms are **diaper dirt, passed away,** and **sanitary engineer.**

every

Every is an indefinite pronoun that is singular and hence takes a singular verb. *Every person I spoke to said she or he was happy.*

every day, everyday

Every day is a noun phrase. *We bathe every day.* **Everyday** is an adjective. *Birth is an everyday occurrence.*

everyone, every one

Everyone means **everybody.** *Everyone enjoyed dinner.* **Every one** means **each.** *Every one of the guests ate too much.*

everyplace, every place, everywhere

Everyplace is a casual substitute for **everywhere** and should be avoided in formal writing. **Every place** is an acceptable term meaning **each place.** *The map had a star for every place we needed to find.*

everything from . . . to . . .

Everything from . . . to . . . is often misused to suggest a complete set or sequence where no such set or sequence exists. The following sentence, for example, is vague and misleading: *Boopsie knows everything from biophysics to Etruscan literature.* Since there is no recognizable range of knowledge that falls between biophysics and Etruscan literature, it is unclear what and how much knowledge Boopsie has. It would be more accurate to say, *Boopsie knows a lot including biophysics and Etruscan literature.*

evoke, invoke
Evoke means **call to mind.** *Snowfall evokes Christmas.* **Invoke** means **summon a spirit** or **suggest the existence of a higher authority.** *Whenever I say I want to be a go-go dancer, he invokes Aunt Fifi, the nun.*

except, accept
See also ACCEPT, EXCEPT.

exceptionable, exceptional
Exceptionable means **generating disagreement.** *Most of us tried to ignore his exceptionable remark.* **Exceptional** means **extraordinary.** *I've seen many dogs that could communicate, but your dog has exceptional persuasive abilities.*

Excessive coordination
Excessive coordination results from the attempt to connect too many independent clauses in a single sentence. While technically not incorrect, excessive coordination results in confusingly or monotonously long sentences. *I wanted to tell you about my dog, and I happened to be in your neighborhood, but I remembered you said you didn't like dogs, and I knew you probably weren't going to be home anyway, so I wrote you a letter about my cat instead.* This sentence would be clearer if it were broken up into two or three sentences or rephrased to make some of the clauses subordinate to others. *Although I wanted to tell you about my dog when I was in your neighborhood, I remembered you don't like dogs. Moreover, I knew you weren't going to be home anyway, so I wrote you a letter about my cat instead.*

Excessive subordination

Excessive subordination results from the attempt to connect too many dependent clauses to a single independent clause, resulting in a sentence that is difficult to understand. *Paying property taxes is especially troublesome for older people, since they increase as property increases in value, even though the property being taxed may have been inexpensive when originally purchased.* This sentence would be clearer if it were broken up into two or more sentences. *Paying property taxes is especially troublesome for older people. These taxes increase as property increases in value even though the property being taxed may have been inexpensive when originally purchased.*

Exclamation point

This punctuation mark (!) used at the end of a sentence to indicate surprise or special intensity. *We're all out of napkins and Mom is coming over!* Writers should avoid using exclamation points to excess.

See also EMPHASIS.

exoteric, esoteric

See also ESOTERIC, EXOTERIC.

Expletive construction

Expletive construction involves the use of the word **it** or **there** at the beginning of a sentence in order to delay introducing the subject. *It is a nice day outside.* Here **it** substitutes for what would be the subject in the more direct sentence, *The day is nice.* Expletive construction is often used casually in ways that are inappropriate to formal writing, resulting in sentences that are unnecessarily wordy and vague. Expletive construction can be useful in formal writing, however, to organize and clarify complicated ideas that cannot be presented all at once. *There are at least six good reasons for planning carefully.*

explicit, implicit
Explicit means stated specifically. **Implicit** means suggested but not stated. *The No Smoking sign explicitly says not to smoke. It implicitly identifies the room as the area in which smoking is not allowed.*

express, expressed
The adjective, **express,** means **definite** or **clear** and generally refers to intentions. *His express purpose in racing competitively is to stay in shape.* **Expressed** is an adjective meaning stated. *His expressed intention was to show off his running shoes, but I think he was trying to lose weight.*

F

factious, factitious, fictitious

Factitious means **constructed** or **made up** and is used to refer to appearances that are misleading or conclusions that are unwarranted. *Her sadness was real, but factitious, since she chose to wallow in self-pity rather than get on with her life.* **Fictitious** means **imaginary.** *Her friend Mel may be fictitious, but she still likes him better than she likes you.* **Factious** means **causing dissent.** *Her factious words nearly caused an argument.*

factitious, fictitious, factious

See also FACTIOUS, FACTITIOUS, FICTITIOUS.

farther, further

Farther means a greater spatial distance. **Further** means a greater temporal distance or greater degree. *The red house is farther away than the blue one. Your drowsiness, coupled with your runny nose, is further evidence that you have a cold.*

fault

Strictly speaking, **Fault** should not be used as a verb meaning **criticize.** *One cannot fault his good intentions.* It is more appropriate to say, *One cannot find fault with* *his good intentions.* Use of **fault** as a verb, however, is now common and acceptable to some authorities.

Faulty coordination

Faulty coordination results when two ideas are brought together as independent clauses that either have no logical relationship or are of unequal importance. *It is hot out today and a new family moved in down the block.* The two independent clauses making up this sentence have no logical connection. The connection needs to be made with information supplied in a whole new clause or sentence. *It is so hot out today that I don't feel like visiting the new family that moved in down the block.*

Faulty coordination also results when one clause is not subordinated properly to another. *It is hot out today and I'm staying inside where it's cooler.* One of the two independent clauses in this sentence should be rewritten as a dependant clause logically subordinate to the other. The sentence should read, *Because it is hot outside I'm staying inside where it's cooler.*

Faulty parallelism

Words and word groups connected by the coordinating conjunction **and** or by the correlative conjunctions **both . . . and, either . . . or,** and **whether . . . or** should take the same grammatical structure. Words and word groups connected by these conjunctions that are structurally different are examples of faulty parallelism. *I like keeping on top of the news and to talk with local politicians.* Here the verb phrases **keeping on top of the news** and **to talk with local politicians** are not parallel in structure. The sentence should read, *I like to keep on* *top of the news and to talk with local politicians,* or, *I like keeping on top of the news and talking with local politicians.*

Faulty predication

Faulty predication is an improper logical relationship between subject and predicate. *The time he spent shaking hands demonstrated his willingness to help.* Here, the subject, **time,** is said to demonstrate willingness, a logically incorrect assertion. A more accurate statement is, *He demonstrated his willingness to help by spending time shaking hands.*

Faulty predication often results from using the subordinating conjunction **because** in a clause that modifies the subject **reason.** *The reason I shake hands is because I want to show my willingness.* This sentence combines a dependent clause with an incomplete independent clause. The sentence should read, *The reason I shake hands is to show my willingness,* or, *I shake hands because I want to show my willingness.*

Faulty Predication
*This is the **reason why** you are hungry. My **belief** in you **turned out to be** a big disappointment. That **recipe** for pancakes **tastes** like cardboard.*

See also REASON BECAUSE, REASON WHY.

fearful, fearsome

Both **fearful** and **fearsome** are used to mean **causing fear. Fearsome,** however, is the more precise term and is therefore preferable. Conversely, **fearful,** and not **fearsome** should be used to mean **afraid.**

few are

Few is a plural indefinite pronoun that requires a plural verb. It is thus grammatically inconsistent to say, *There is only a few seats left.*

fewer, less

Fewer is an adjective that should be used with count nouns, those nouns that designate things that can be counted, whether the noun is singular or plural. *There are fewer birds than there used to be. There is one fewer bird in the cage.*

Less is an adjective that should be used with mass nouns and abstractions. *The new cars use less gas. They are less trouble to start.*

In general, **fewer** is appropriate to refer to things that can be numbered. Quantified amounts such as time, weight, or volume, however, should usually be used with **less**, even when they are numbered. *She weighs less than 100 pounds.* It takes less time to get to *The state line from Main Street than from Oak Avenue.* Use of **less** in this way is actually not an exception to the general rule, since it modifies not the number, but the amount, even though the word designating amount may not be stated in the sentence. *She weighs less [weight] than 100 pounds.* When numbers rather than amounts are referred to, the appropriate adjective is **fewer.** *I weigh five fewer pounds.* Contrast *I weigh five pounds less.*

fiancé, fiancée

A fiancé is a groom-to-be. A fiancée is a bride-to-be.

fictitious, factitious, factious

See also FACTIOUS, FACTITIOUS, FICTITIOUS.

Figurative language

Figurative, as opposed to literal, language conveys meaning in special ways, especially metaphorically or ironically, by using words other than in their denotative senses.

See also LITERAL LANGUAGE, IRONY, and METAPHOR.

finalize

Finalize is a neologism that should be avoided in formal discourse. Use conclude or complete instead.

See also NEOLOGISM.

First person

First person is the classification of pronouns including I and me in the singular and we and us in the plural. A narrative written in the first person is a narrative written about oneself from one's own point of view. Contrast SECOND PERSON and THIRD PERSON.

Some readers object to the use of the first person in expository writing as unnecessarily intimate. Indeed, referring to oneself may diminish the cogency of an objective presentation of ideas. *After reviewing the facts, I feel that assault weapons are dangerous.* Here, the first person pronoun makes the feeling described less persuasive than it might otherwise be, because it identifies the writer's position as mere opinion, rather than as a reasoned discussion intended to make others understand a problem more clearly.

Use of I and other first person pronouns in formal

writing, however, is not necessarily wrong. Offering personal experiences to illustrate a discussion can be especially persuasive. *I was nearly shot by an assault rifle. The experience continues to give me nightmares. We must ban these guns.*

See also **OBJECTIVITY.**

firstly

Firstly, secondly, and so forth are nonstandard sentence modifiers that should be avoided in formal writing. Instead use **first, second,** etc.

See also **SENTENCE MODIFIERS.**

fish, fishes

Properly, the plural of **fish** is simply **fish. Fishes** should be used to refer not simply to more than one fish but to more than one kind of fish. *The pet shop sells even the most exotic fishes.*

flagrant, blatant

See also **BLATANT, FLAGRANT.**

flair, flare

Only **flair** should be used to refer to personal talent. *She has a flair for sword-swallowing.* **Flare** means **shine brightly** or **burst into flames** and may be used figuratively with **up** to refer to any sudden event or emotion. *Her ulcers flare up from time to time.*

flammable, inflammable

The two words mean the same thing, **easily ignited,** in spite of the difference in spelling.

flare, flair

See also FLAIR, FLARE.

flaunt, flout

These words, often confused, have very different meanings. **Flaunt** means **display prominently.** *He drove to the park simply to flaunt his new sports car.* **Flout** means **ignore or break rules.** *The beachcombers routinely flout the law against building fires on the beach.*

flounder, founder

Flounder and **founder** are both verbs having to do with unsuccessful moving or standing. **Flounder** usually applies to people and means **move clumsily with struggle.** **Founder** usually applies to ships, buildings, or horses and means **sink, cave in,** or **go lame.** Used figuratively, **founder** may be used to refer to ideas. *When you get to your discussion of enthusiasm, your argument founders.*

Focus

The focus of a piece of writing is the scope or breadth of the ideas it discusses. The focus should be established at the beginning by means of a general presentation of the more specific ideas to come. It should not be so general, however, that it refers to ideas not discussed in the work.

See also THESIS.

follows

See also AS FOLLOWS.

for free, for real, for sure

The preposition **for** is colloquial and unnecessary when it precedes **free, real,** or **sure.** In formal writing, it is inappropriate to say, *We got the supplies for free.* It is preferable to say, *The supplies were free,* or, *We got the supplies for nothing.*

forceful, forcible

Forceful means **powerful** or **effective.** *She has a forceful argument.* **Forcible** means **coercive** or **violent.** *The guards made forcible searches of anyone they suspected of having concealed weapons.*

Formality

Formal writing is not ideally more pretentious and obscure than ordinary communication, but it is more precise and articulate. It may be ceremonial in tone, but it certainly does not need to be. The crucial difference between formal writing and ordinary speech is that formal writing deals with subjects that are more complex than the mundane subjects of informal exchanges. Therefore, to present complex material clearly and accurately, it is necessary to use words that have exact, specific meanings and to arrange them into grammatical structures that make them as easy to understand as possible.

The distinguishing features of good formal writing are a thesis or main purpose clearly stated or implied; words used precisely and with specificity; and a flexible and varied use of grammatical structure so as to organize concepts intelligibly and without monotony. These features are means to an end. They help convey ideas and information for which style alone is no substitute.

Some authorities assert that the personal pronoun **I** should be avoided in formal writing. It is unnecessary to qualify one's ideas with phrases such as **I think, I feel,** or **I have found,** since experienced readers know that all writing is produced by human beings who call themselves **I** and who are fallible. Humility is unnecessary and any uncertainty should be acknowledged and assessed in a more direct manner than by hiding behind an **I.** The **I,** however, should not be ruled out of formal discourse. Good formal writing does not result from following rules but from making intelligent choices.

former

Former should be used to identify the first in a comparison between two things. Thus it is incorrect to say, *Of mushrooms, pepperoni, and anchovies, I prefer the former.* **First-mentioned** is a more appropriate term here.

See also LAST NAMED, LATTER.

fortunate, fortuitous

Fortunate is an adjective used to describe people. **Fortuitous** is an adjective used to describe events. Thus it is inaccurate to say, *Our meeting was a fortunate occurrence.* It is more appropriate to say, *Our meeting was a fortuitous occurrence.*

founder, flounder

See also FLOUNDER, FOUNDER.

Fragments

Sentences are generally said to be fragments if they lack a predicate. *Leaves turning aimlessly in the wind. To run until you feel your heart in your throat.* These clauses have no predicate. Sentences without a stated subject are not considered fragments if they are commands. *Wash the dishes.* Here the subject, **you,** is implied.

Fragments are generally considered unacceptable, although they are often used effectively to suggest emotion or meditation.

free gift
A gift is free by definition. The phrase free gift is therefore redundant and should be avoided.

See also **REDUNDANCY.**

from . . . to . . .
See also **EVERYTHING FROM . . . TO . . .**

from whence
From is unnecessary when used with **whence** and should be omitted. *Whence came these discount coupons? Send them back whence they came.*

full, fulsome
Full may be used in either a positive or negative sense. **Fulsome,** however, should only be used as a negative term meaning **excessive and insincere.** *His fulsome encomiums of great writers made us glad they invented television.*

further, farther
See also **FARTHER, FURTHER.**

Fused participles
Nouns are sometimes fused with participles when they should take the possessive case to distinguish them from

the participle. *We celebrated Shana getting a promotion.*
Here **Shana** is fused with the participle, **getting.** The sentence should read, *We celebrated Shana's getting a promotion.*

See also **PARTICIPLES** and **POSSESSIVE CASE.**

Fused sentences
Also called run-on sentences, fused sentences are two
distinct sentences that are not separated by periods but
joined, usually by a comma. *I like you, you are my
friend.* Here two distinct sentences are fused. Fused
sentences are errors and should be avoided.

Future perfect progressive tense
The future progressive is the verb tense indicating
ongoing actions taking place at a specific time in the future. It is made by adding **will have been** to the gerund
-ing form of the verb. *I will have been working all day
by the time you come over.*

Future perfect tense
The future perfect is the verb tense indicating actions to
be completed by a specified time in the future. It is
made by adding **will have** to the past participle **-ed** form
of the verb. *I will have repaired the fence by the time
you bring the alligator.*

Future progressive tense
The future progressive is the verb tense indicating a
continuous action in the future. It is made by adding
will be to the gerund **-ing** form of the verb. *We'll be
elsewhere when the alligator is escaping.*

Future tense

The future tense indicates an action that takes place in the future. Different future tenses are **simple future, future progressive, future perfect,** and **future perfect progressive.**

G

Gender

Gender is a way of classifying nouns and pronouns. They can be feminine, masculine, or neuter. Feminine nouns are **woman, girl,** proper names given to women, and the words for the female of a species of animals such as **cow** or **doe.** Other feminine nouns indicating occupations such as **waitress** and **stewardess** are becoming obsolete and are usually considered inappropriate. Feminine nouns take the feminine pronouns, **she, her,** and **hers.**

Masculine nouns are **man, boy,** proper names given to men, and the words for the male of a species of animals such as **bull** or **buck.** They take the masculine pronouns, **he, him,** and **his.**

Nouns and pronouns that are neither feminine nor masculine are neuter. In English, most nouns are neuter, including **cigar, keyhole,** and **beauty.** Neuter nouns take the neuter pronouns, **it** and **its.**

Traditionally, male pronouns have been used generically to refer to nouns that may designate either male or female things, or both. This practice is generally considered inappropriate and should be avoided.

See also GENERIC HE.

gender, sex

Gender and **sex** are often confused. **Gender** refers to the way things are classified. **Sex** refers to the manner in which people and animals reproduce. Thus it is mistaken to say *The names of hurricanes may be of either the masculine or feminine sex.* The appropriate word here is **gender.** It is also mistaken to say, *All the students in the sewing class were of the masculine gender.* The appropriate word here is **sex.**

General terms

General terms, as opposed to specific terms, designate things in a broad manner. They are less precise but more inclusive. **Road,** for example, is a general term whose meaning includes the more specific terms, **street, highway, drive, avenue,** etc. Although specific terms are often preferable to general terms since they are more precise and vivid, too much specificity regarding unimportant things can focus attention where it does not belong.

Generic he

The generic he is the male pronoun **he,** used to refer to nouns that designate both males and females. *Every corporate executive wants to be richer than he already is.* Because corporate executives are both male and female, it is inaccurate to refer to this group with the male pronoun **he.** Traditionally, however, **he** has been used in this way, although this practice has generally become unacceptable. The sentence may be revised in any of a number of ways: *All corporate executives want to be richer than they already are,* or, *Every corporate execu-*

tive wants to be richer than he or she already is, or,
*Every corporate executive wants to be richer than
he/she already is.* An unacceptable alternative is the use
of the plural pronoun **their** to refer to the singular noun,
every. It is incorrect in formal writing to say, *Every corporate executive wants to be richer than they already
are.*

Genitive case

The genitive case is the form of nouns in Latin that is
used to show ownership or pertinence. The term **genitive case** is sometimes used to refer to the possessive
case in English.

See also POSSESSIVE CASE.

Gerund phrases

Gerund phrases serve as nouns. They are based on verbs
ending in **-ing.** *Spearfishing without sufficient experience can be dangerous.* Here, **spearfishing without
sufficient experience** is a gerund phrase based on the
gerund, **spearfishing.**

Gerunds

Gerunds are verb forms ending in **-ing** that are used as
nouns. *Swimming is good for you.*

get

Get and other forms of the verb, **to get** are often
overused and should be avoided where more precise,
specific verbs are available. *The ground is getting worn
away where toxic runoff has killed the plants..* This sentence could be revised to read, *The ground is eroding
where toxic runoff has killed the plants.* There is nothing

wrong grammatically, however, with using **get** or **got** to mean **become,** as well as **own,** or **acquire.**

good, well

Good, an adjective, and **well,** an adverb, are often misused. **Good** should be used to modify nouns. *The peace rally was good.* **Good** should not be used to modify verbs. It is therefore incorrect to say, *I'm doing good.* One should instead say, *I'm doing well.*

Some grammarians assert that it is similarly incorrect to say **I feel good,** rather than **I feel well. I feel good,** however, is acceptable since **good** may be understood to serve as the complement of the subject, **I,** rather than as an adverb modifying the verb, **feel.** Although **good** should not be used as an adverb modifying **feel,** it may be used as the subject complement of **I.**

See also **SUBJECT COMPLEMENTS.**

got, have

Got, the past tense form of the verb, **to get,** is often used informally after **have,** and sometimes in place of **have,** to mean **must.** *I have got to get an umbrella,* or, *I got to get an umbrella*. While **have got** is widely accepted, **got** by itself is considered incorrect, although both are inappropriate in formal discourse. **Must** is more suitable.

Grammar

Grammar, as opposed to usage, is a set of rules governing the structure of language. Traditionally, the study of English grammar has been based on Latin grammar, which is more complicated. All Latin nouns, for example, unlike English nouns, are gendered and must be sorted out into five cases. English, in contrast, only has three cases, one of which, the subjunctive, is almost never used. Rather than putting a different ending on every noun, the English language uses separate words to indicate the noun's function. Moreover, the order in which words appear in English sentences is more predictable than in Latin and often indicates the function of words, so that different case endings are less necessary.

Better awareness of grammar promotes more accurate, persuasive, and engaging prose. Improving one's grammar does not simply mean memorizing a lot of rules in order to write correctly. Instead, it means understanding language as a shared technology, one that is subject to change and variation, but one that requires agreement—agreement among people as well as between subjects and verbs and between pronouns and antecedents.

Grammar is, in part, a matter of accuracy and precision. Those who use bad grammar often end up saying things that are not literally true, as in a sentence that uses a subject case pronoun instead of an object pronoun. Such sentences are not so much wrong, however, as sloppy. Sloppiness can be a source of enjoyment for many and such enjoyment of sloppiness sometimes becomes incorporated into accepted practice in spite of grammatical rules that may say a given construction is wrong. Thus usage and accepted idioms may contradict and even supersede the so-called rules of grammar.

See also **IDIOMS**.

grateful, gratified
Grateful and **gratified** are similar in meaning in that they both refer to a pleasurable feeling in response to

beneficial events. **Grateful,** however, refers specifically
to feelings toward other people or personified forces
who have benefited us. **Grateful** implies thankfulness
for benefits that may or may not have been expected. *We
are grateful for your good advice.* **Gratified,** unlike
grateful, does not imply a distinction between the cause
of the benefit and the satisfaction derived from it. It
refers to benefits that are expected or hoped for. *We
were gratified that our plans worked out s...."*

grisly, grizzled, grizzly

Grisly means **gruesome** or **terrifying.** *More and more
movies for young people are grisly in the extreme.* **Grizzly** or **grizzled** means gray in color and is used most
often to refer to hair or fur. **Grizzly,** of course, is also a
kind of bear.

H

hail, hale

Hail and **hale** are sometimes confused. **Hail** as a verb means **greet** or **salute**. *They hailed us as we got off the plane.* As a noun, hail also means icy rain. **Hale** means **force to go.** *They handcuffed us and haled us into their police cars.* **Hale** also means **healthy.**

hanged, hung

Hanged and **hung** are past tense forms of **hang.** **Hanged** is used specifically in reference to executions. **Hung** is used in all other cases. *In the seventeenth century, criminals were hanged in public. Children hung from trees to get a better view.*

hardly

Hardly has the effect of negating whatever it modifies. As a result, it should not be used with other negatives, as in the phrases, **not hardly, hardly never,** and **hardly no.**

See also DOUBLE NEGATIVES.

hardy, hearty

Hardy means **capable of enduring hardship.** *They were so hardy they found boot camp enjoyable.* **Hearty**

means **sincere** and **unrestrained**. *They were so hearty they made everyone feel at ease.*

have, got
See also GOT, HAVE.

have, of
See also COULD HAVE, OF.

healthy, healthful
Healthy is an adjective used to describe people and other living things that are in good physical condition. **Healthful** is used to describe food and activities that promote health. Thus it is inaccurate to call food healthy instead of healthful.

hearty, hardy
See also HARDY, HEARTY.

he/she
He/she, she/he, his/her and **her/his** are acceptable alternatives to the generic **he** or **his** used as a pronoun to refer nouns that may be either male or female. *Everyone came with his/her own set of utensils.* Also acceptable is **he or she, she or he, her or his,** etc.

See also GENERIC HE and INCLUSIVE LANGUAGE.

Helping verbs
See also AUXILIARY VERBS.

hisself, himself
Hisself is a nonstandard form of the reflexive pronoun, **himself.** *After the scolding, the dog kept to hisself.* **His-**

self is unacceptable in standard English. The sentence should read, *After the scolding the dog kept to himself.*

historic, historical

Historic refers to things that are famous. **Historical** refers to things concerned with the study of history. *Important events took place in this historic building. It has a historical annex where records are kept.*

hoard, horde

A hoard is a stash or large supply of money or valuables. It may be used as a verb. *We discovered it was a mistake to hoard toilet paper rather than food.* A horde is a huge crowd of warlike people. It may be used figuratively to refer to any large group of people or animals. *A horde of librarians descended upon Spokane for the annual conference.*

homogenous, homogeneous

Homogenous means **coming from the same background.** *Most ghettos are homogenous.* **Homogeneous** means **having similar characteristics.** *Most middle-class neighborhoods are homogeneous.*

Homonym

A homonym is a word that sounds like another word, such as **deer** and **dear.** Obviously, the meanings differ.

hopefully

Hopefully is properly used as an adverb to mean **with hope.** *We listened hopefully to the message.* It is often used as a sentence modifier, however, to mean **one**

hopes. *Hopefully, tomorrow will be sunny.* This second use of **hopefully** is less acceptable.

See also **SENTENCE MODIFIERS.**

horde, hoard

See also **HOARD, HORDE.**

hundred, hundreds

Hundred may be used in the plural to refer to a specific number of hundreds. Hundreds is used for an estimated number. *The theater holds hundreds of people. Two hundred bought tickets for this evening's performance.*

Hung paragraph

A hung paragraph is a block of quoted text that has wider margins to distinguish it from the rest of the text. Hung paragraphs should be at least three lines long. Shorter quotations should be placed within quotation marks. Quotations that are set off in hung paragraphs should not be further set off by quotation marks. Hung paragraphs may or may not be separated from the rest of the text by skipping a line beforehand and afterward.

Hyphens

Hyphens (-) should be used to divide words between syllables when they will not fit at the end of a line of words. They should not divide syllables and they should not isolate syllables that are only one or two letters long.

Hyphens are also used to connect compound adjectives: words that are joined into a single modifier of a noun such as **state-of-the-art technology** or **heat-seeking missile.** Hyphens need not be used when the modifier follows the noun. The technology was state of the art.

Hyphens are also used when spelling out fractions such as two-thirds and one-fifth and for spelling out compound numbers such as forty-four and seventy-two.

Hyphens may also be used to indicate that a word has been interrupted, as in **pre- and postwar** and **un- and overenthusiastic.**

Some prefixes, but not all, should be joined to main words by means of a suffix. A hyphen should be used with the prefixes **all-, self-,** and **ex-** when it is used to mean **former.** Hyphens should also be used in other cases when they add clarity, such as **co-opt,** and **mother-in-law-elect.**

I

I

I may be used in expository writing whenever it is necessary for the writer to explain something about her- or himself, or when examples from personal experience are used to help clarify or illustrate a discussion. **I** should be avoided when its use simply qualifies the ideas presented as in the phrases, **I think, I feel,** and **I believe.**

See also **FIRST PERSON.**

-ics

Words ending in -ics such as *politics, calisthenics, acoustics,* etc., may be either plural or singular nouns. They are singular when they refer to a general art or study. In such cases, they take singular verbs. *Acrobatics is a dangerous profession.* They are plural when they refer to specific instances of the general practice. *Your acrobatics are amusing.*

See also **POLITICS** and **STATISTICS.**

ideology, knowledge

Both **ideology** and **knowledge** are used to refer to organized ideas that are accepted as true by the people who have them. **Ideology,** unlike **knowledge,** implies that these ideas are not simply true, but obscure hidden assumptions subject to analysis and criticism on ethical and political grounds.

When people speak of knowledge, they usually do so with the assumption that language is a reliable source of objective meaning. They also assume that people are intelligent insofar as they are innately capable of gaining and using knowledge. In contrast, when people speak of ideology, they recognize knowledge as having an uncertain relationship to language and individuality, that language, constituted as knowledge, influences people in different ways by facilitating and encouraging certain kinds of actions and beliefs and restricting others.

See also DISCOURSE, LANGUAGE and SELF, SUBJECTIVITY.

Idioms

Idioms are accepted constructions that do not obey grammatical rules. Idioms cannot be translated literally into other languages. Some idiomatic expressions are **bring down the house, hold up your end of the bargain,** and **by and large.**

Many prepositions are idiomatic and present difficulty even to native speakers of English. Prepositions accompanying the verb, **agree,** for example, are often confused. *We agree to the proposal. We agree with the president. We agree on the plan.*

See also PREPOSITIONS.

i.e., e.g.

See also E.G., I.E.

if, whether

Both **if** and **whether** introduce adverb clauses. **If** should be used to present a possibility; **whether** should be used to present a choice between two possibilities. *If I don't snore, how will you know whether I'm asleep?* In formal writing, **if** should not be used where a choice between two things is being presented. It is inaccurate, for example, to say, *Let me know if you decide to come or not.* It is preferable to say, *Let me know whether you decide to come.* The phrase, **or not** may be included immediately after **whether** or it may be omitted.

illicit, elicit

See also ELICIT, ILLICIT.

illusion, allusion

See also ALLUSION, ILLUSION.

illusion, delusion

See also DELUSION, ILLUSION.

immanent, imminent, eminent

See also EMINENT, IMMANENT, IMMINENT.

immoral, amoral

See also AMORAL, IMMORAL.

impact

Although **impact** is frequently used as a verb meaning **influence,** such usage is incorrect. **Impact** is properly a noun, not a verb. One should not say, *The new director may impact our project adversely.* It is more acceptable to say, *The new director may have an adverse impact on our project.* Even as a noun, however, **impact** is often overused. Although it has an analytical connotation, it is a general term that should be avoided wherever a more specific term is available. It is more informative, for example, to say, *The new director will misallocate funding for our project.*

Imperative mood
The imperative is the verb mood used for commands, as opposed to the declarative or indicative mood and the subjunctive mood. In English, the imperative mood takes the same form as the declarative. Often, however, the subject, **you,** is implied rather than stated. *Clean up that nuclear waste!*

See also **MOOD OF VERB.**

implicit, explicit
See also **EXPLICIT, IMPLICIT.**

imply, infer
Imply and **infer** are commonly used indiscriminately, although they have different meanings. Both verbs are used with subjects having to do with unstated ideas, but **imply** means **suggest** or **involve** whereas infer means **gather** or **deduce.** *When he said he had tasted better fatback ribs, he implied that he did not think the high price was fair. We inferred that he did not appreciate the special ambiance of Greasy Granny's Rib Kitchen.*

important, importantly
Important should be used rather than **importantly** as a sentence modifier. *More important, air travel will remain safe.*

See also SENTENCE MODIFIERS.

in back of
In back of is used colloquially to mean **behind,** but it should be avoided in formal writing.

in behalf of, on behalf of
See also BEHALF.

incisive, decisive
See also DECISIVE, INCISIVE.

Inclusive language
Inclusive language is language that avoids using the male pronouns, **he, him,** and **his,** as well as other words such as **mankind** generically to refer to people who may be either men or women. Traditionally, many terms for professions, as well as other work-related words, have reflected the biased assumption that men do only certain kinds of jobs and women do others. Such terms, including **salesman, stewardess, anchorman, housewife,** and **manpower,** are misleading and inappropriate given the desirability of equal job opportunities for women and men. Instead, terms such as **salesperson, flight attendant, newscaster, homemaker,** and **workforce** may be used.

See also BIASED LANGUAGE, and GENERIC HE, and HE/SHE.

Incomplete comparison

An incomplete comparison is a phrase that suggests something is going to be compared to something else, but the phrase doesn't mention the second term. *My fingers are so sore.* Incomplete comparisons should be avoided in formal writing. Many incomplete comparisons occur in sentences that use the word **than.** *Gervis is taller when he wears his new shoes than his sneakers.* Incomplete comparisons also result from using **such** or **so** as terms of emphasis rather than as terms of comparison. *You are so lucky. You have such good luck.* Incomplete comparison is also a familiar advertising technique. Many ads use comparative terms such as **more** and **bigger** without presenting two terms for comparison. *You get more out of our product.*

> ### *Incomplete Comparisons*
> *Dogs can be such a nuisance. Our brand of medicine works faster. Playing soccer in your neighborhood is more fun than mine.*

See also COMPARISON; SO; SUCH; and THAN, THEN.

Incomplete construction

Incomplete constructions result when a sentence does not say what it was intended to say because it lacks information. This happens most often with comparisons. *The road that runs by your house is safer than ours.* Here the comparison is an incomplete construction since it does not make the intended comparison of one road to another but compares the road to a house.

Another form of incomplete construction occurs when dependant clauses are not subordinated to an independent clause. Dependent clauses that appear by themselves are sentence fragments: *When you get rid of your grasshopper, Because I need my teeth for chewing, If we don't get arrested for indecent exposure.*

See also **DEPENDENT CLAUSES; FRAGMENTS;** and **INCOMPLETE COMPARISON.**

Incomplete sentence
See also **FRAGMENTS.**

Inconsistency
See also **CONSISTENCY.**

Indefinite articles
The indefinite articles are **a** and **an.** In contrast to the definite article, **the,** indefinite articles indicate general nouns. *A can opener may be large or small.*

See also **Articles** and **Definite articles.**

Indefinite pronouns
Indefinite pronouns refer to nouns but not to specific things. Examples are **all, any, each, either, every, neither, none, nothing, one,** and **some.** Indefinite pronouns are usually singular and take a singular verb. *Each of us has different quirks.* **Nothing** is always singular. However, **both, few,** and **many** are plural. *Many are in need of assistance.* Many indefinite pronouns, including **all, any, most,** and **some** can take either a singular or a plural verb depending on the context. *All I ask is that you listen. All my feelings are confused.*

Indefinite pronouns should not be inflected for possession unless they end in **-one** or **-body.** It is acceptable to say, *Is this anybody's grease spot?* It is incorrect to say, *It could be either's, all's, most's, both's, etc.*

See also **COLLECTIVE NOUNS; POSSESSIVE CASE;** and **PRONOUNS.**

Indefinite subjects

Indefinite pronouns can function as the subjects of some sentences. Whether they take a plural or singular verb depends on whether the noun they refer to is singular or plural.

See also **INDEFINITE PRONOUNS.**

Independent clauses

An independent clause contains a subject and a verb and requires no additional information in order to constitute a complete sentence. It may, however, be combined with other clauses to form longer sentences. *I'm too hungry to sleep.* This independent clause can be joined with other clauses. *Although I'm tired, I'm too hungry to sleep.* Here the independent clause is preceded by a dependent clause. *I'm too hungry to sleep, and my feet hurt.* Here the independent clause is followed by another independent clause.

See also **CLAUSES** and **SENTENCES.**

Indicative mood

See also **DECLARATIVE MOOD.**

Indirect discourse

Indirect discourse reports what was said without stating exact words. *I told the kids they could stay up late tonight.* Contrast direct discourse: *I told the kids, "You can stay up late tonight."*

Indirect objects

Indirect objects are placed after transitive verbs and before direct objects. They typically answer the questions, **to whom, for whom,** and **to what.** *Give me the water balloon.* Here, **me** is the indirect object, **give** is a transitive verb, and **water balloon** is the direct object. When indirect objects are pronouns, they take the object case.

See also CASE and OBJECT CASE.

Indirect questions

Indirect questions report, rather than ask questions. They should end with periods rather than question marks. *I asked how her kidneys were feeling. She wondered what business that was of mine.*

individual, person

Individual may be used to refer to a single member of a group. *The rules are intended to restrict the freedom of the individual as little as possible.* **Individual** should not be used in the more general sense as a synonym for **person,** even where eccentricity or uniqueness is implied. *She is a delightful and unusual person.*

inequity, iniquity

Inequity means **injustice.** *We must continue to resist inequity in publicly funded education.* **Iniquity** means **immorality.** *His money did not turn him into a bad person, although he used it to hide his iniquity.*

infer, imply

See also IMPLY, INFER.

Infinitives

Infinitives are main verb forms preceded by **to,** such as **to eat, to do,** and **to be.** They can be used as nouns, as adverbs, and as adjectives. *To wander aimlessly for hours is to get a good workout.* Here the infinitives, **to wander** and **to get** are used as nouns. Infinitives can also be used as adjectives. *You must resist the urge to sit down.* Here the infinitive, **to sit down** is an adjective modifying the noun, **urge.**

Traditionally, it has been considered improper to split infinitives by inserting modifiers between **to** and the verb. Split infinitives, however, are becoming acceptable to greater numbers of readers. *I prefer to only walk a few miles at a time.* Some readers, however, continue to object to split infinitives.

inflammable, flammable

See also FLAMMABLE, INFLAMMABLE.

Inflated diction

Inflated diction occurs when unusual words are selected fatuously for their intellectual connotations rather than because they are more precise than more ordinary words. Though it may impress inexperienced readers, it is more likely to bore them. It reveals to experienced readers the intellectual limitations and foolish presumptions of the writer.

See also DICTION.

Inflection

Inflection is the changing of the various parts of speech into different forms. In English, verbs may be inflected according to whether they are singular or plural, according to their mood, and according to person. Most nouns may be inflected as either singular or plural and as either subjective or possessive. Pronouns can be inflected as singular or plural and as subjective, possessive, or objective.

Many adjectives can be inflected as adverbs by adding the suffix, **-ly.** Some adjectives can be inflected as nouns by adding the suffixes, **-ness** or **-ity.** The gerund verb form inflects verbs as nouns by adding the suffix **-ing.**

In written English, the parts of speech are not inflected differently for questions and statements, but in spoken English, questions and statements have an audible inflection. Compare the question, *She arrived last night?* with the statement, *She arrived last night.*

In addition to inflection, word order and meaning help distinguish the different functions of the various parts of speech.

ingenious, ingenuous
Ingenious means **brilliant** or **clever.** *It was an ingenious solution to the problem.* **Ingenuous** means **guileless, sincere,** or **frank.** *Your questions about her awards were too flattering to be ingenuous.*

iniquity, inequity
See also **INEQUITY, INIQUITY.**

input as noun and verb
Input is originally a specialized noun meaning information entered into a computer. It has become widely used to mean an opinion contributed to a discussion. *We're*

talking about Mitch's hairdo and we'd love to hear your input. **Input** should not be used as a verb. It is incorrect to say, *The alphabet soup will be ready as soon as I input a few more letters.* **Enter** is a more suitable word to refer to the process of adding information to a computer file. **Add** is appropriate in other cases.

in regards to

In regards to is a colloquial substitute for **in regard to** that should be avoided in formal writing.

insure, assure, ensure

See also ASSURE, ENSURE, INSURE.

Intensifiers

Intensifiers are adverbs and adjectives that are used to emphasize the words they modify, such as **actually, certainly, truly,** and **very.**

Interjections

Interjections are words or phrases added as exclamations, such as **Dad blast it, Jiminy Cricket, glory be, oh, ouch,** and **rats.** They may occur anywhere within a sentence or as separate sentences.

Interrogative pronouns

Interrogative pronouns are those used in questions. They include **how, who, whom, whose, where,** and **which.**

Intransitive verbs

Intransitive verbs are verbs that do not take objects. The action they describe is not directed to anything other

than the subject. *The cows moo. The children sleep.*
Contrast transitive verbs that take objects. *The cows eat
clover. The children throw eggs.* Intransitive verbs can
be used as transitive verbs when they have an effect on
the subject so that the subject reflexively becomes its
own object. *The cows moo themselves to sleep. The
children sleep away their cares.*

Intransitive verbs are sometimes used incorrectly as
transitive verbs. *The coach evolved his team.*

> **Incorrect Transitive Verbs**
> *The boss **resigned** his employee. The artist **emerged** his
> new painting. He **languished** his tennis game. The stu-
> dents **blossomed** their abilities.*

See also **TRANSITIVE VERBS.**

Introductory elements
Introductory elements are words and phases that come
before the main clause in a sentence including words
such as **well, indeed,** and **incidentally**; prepositional
phrases such as **in case of emergency**; verbal phrases
such as **having eaten four chocolate eclairs**; and dependent clauses such as **when the wind blows.** Introductory elements should be followed by a comma.

invaluable, valuable
Invaluable does not mean the opposite of **valuable,** but
means **extremely valuable** or **priceless.**

invoke, evoke
See also **EVOKE, INVOKE.**

Irony

Irony is figurative language that makes assertions contrary to what it implies. More broadly, it is anything that happens contrary to what is expected. *The elephant tiptoed daintily through the strawberry patch. I love lawyers; they are remarkably agreeable and accepting.*

The word **irony** is sometimes misused to mean **significant** or **coincidental,** especially by sports commentators attempting to make random events and meaningless statistics seem interesting. Although all ironic events may be said to have significance and may be coincidental, not all significant or coincidental events are ironic. Thus it is unacceptable to say, *How ironic that player number nine hit nine home runs this season!* We might say instead, *How ironic that professional commentators don't know the meaning of the word, irony!*

irregardless

Irregardless is a nonstandard variant of **regardless.** Now a famous example of bogus usage, **irregardless** is unacceptable unless used for comic effect.

Irregular verbs

Irregular verbs are verbs whose past tense and past participle are not formed by adding **-d** or **-ed** to the end of the present tense form as with most English verbs. The most commonly used irregular verbs are **be, do,** and **have,** whose present and past tense forms are **are, were, do, did,** and **have, had,** respectively. Contrast the regular verb, **hope, hoped.** Some other irregular verbs include **bend, bent, catch, caught,** and **know, knew.**

irrelevant, relevant
Irrelevant and **relevant** are often used imprecisely as synonyms for **unimportant** and **important.** Strictly speaking, however, they should be used to show whether something relates to something else. Thus it is imprecise to say, *Your ideas are irrelevant,* since this is an incomplete comparison. It is more appropriate to say, *Your ideas are irrelevant to my interests,*

irritate, aggravate
See also AGGRAVATE, IRRITATE.

is when, is where
Is when and **is where** are constructions that are often used erroneously in sentences that define terms. *Diplomacy is when you persuade others to do what you want them to. Litigation is where you force them to do it.* These sentences are faulty and should be revised: *Diplomacy is the art of persuading others to do what you want them to do. Litigation is the art of forcing them to do it.* **Is when** and **is where** should not be used to explain terms unless the terms are times or places. It is acceptable to say, *Four o'clock is when the English have tea. England is where we went last summer.*

it
It is a pronoun that is often used with insufficient accuracy to refer to other words and phrases. *Wishing the mail would come, I imagined I was trying to clear the snow off the driveway. It was a tedious thing to be doing.* Here it is unclear to what the **it** is supposed to refer. Such ambiguity is known as vague pronoun reference. **It** should not be used unless it refers clearly

and specifically to a word or phrase nearby. The problem may be amended by specifying the reference: *This waiting for the mail was a tedious thing to be doing.*

Italics

Italics is the slanted font used for emphasis. *Do you need to go to the bathroom?* Italics are also used to indicate the titles of books and films.

its, it's

Its is the possessive case of the pronoun, **it**. **It's** is a contraction made from the words, **it is.** These forms are often confused with one another, since the possessive case of most pronouns is formed by adding **'s. Its** is an exception to this rule so that it may be distinguished from the contraction, **it's.** *It's a long way for the rat to go before it gets its food.*

J

Jargon

Jargon is specialized, technical terminology used by groups of professionals but not ordinarily by the general public. Although unnecessary jargon should be avoided, technical terms can be indispensable to those who are familiar with them. For example, the sentence, *The consensus of all affiliated parties was that the binary laws should assimilate the ratification of equalized structure among labor,* might better be stated for the layperson as, *The group agreed that both plans should divide the workload evenly.*

Joining words

See also CONJUNCTIONS.

judicial, judicious

Judicial is an adjective used to modify things having to do with judging. *His judicial attitude often made people think he was impartial.* **Judicious** means **fair** or **just**. *It is difficult to reach a judicious settlement in many divorce cases.*

K

Key words

Key words are generally the nouns and verbs that seem most important in a sentence, a paragraph, or an entire text. It is useful to be aware of key words in one's own writing so as to establish clear transitions between ideas. Also, when quoting, it is useful to use key words from the quotation in showing how the quoted material relates to the topic at hand.

kind, sort, type

Kind, sort, and **type** are collective nouns that take singular verbs unless they are changed to the plural form. Generally, they should be used with a singular noun regardless of whether or not they are plural. *This kind of snake travels rapidly over sand.* Here, **kind** is singular and modifies the singular noun, **snake,** and takes the singular verb, **travels.** *These types of bite are deadly.* Here, the plural pronoun, **types,** modifies the singular noun, **bite** and takes the plural verb form, **are.**

The nouns to which these pronouns refer may be plural only if they precede the pronouns. *Bites of this sort are deadly.* Use of **kind of** and **sort of** to mean **rather** or **partially** should be avoided in formal speech and writing. Such constructions are too casual: *At that point, the British troops were sort of tired of having to* *deal with the revolutionaries.* This sentence should be revised: *At that point, the British troops were growing tired of having to deal with the revolutionaries.*

In formal writing, **kind of, sort of,** and **type of** should not be modified by adjectives that merely characterize, but do not define them. Thus it is lax to say, *The pangolin is an odd sort of animal.* It is acceptable, however, to say *Philbert is an animal of the feline sort.*

knowledge, ideology

See also IDEOLOGY, KNOWLEDGE.

kudos

Kudos, meaning praise, is a singular noun and should take a singular verb form. *The kudos we received for our efforts was gratifying.* The word **kudo** is an erroneous back-formation used by those who mistakenly think **kudos** is plural.

See also BACK-FORMATION.

L

lack in, lack for

Lack usually requires no preposition. Where **lack** takes a preposition, **in** is the proper preposition to use, not **for.** *Whatever you lack in food supplies will be provided.* **Lack for** is nonstandard and should be avoided.

language, discourse

See also DISCOURSE, LANGUAGE.

last-named, latter

Last-named may be used to refer to the final term of a series of three or more. **Latter** may be used to refer to the second of two terms.

See also FORMER.

lay, lie

Lay and **lie** are frequently confused. **Lay** is a transitive verb meaning **place lengthwise on a horizontal surface.** *We lay our assault rifles on the kitchen table.* As a transitive verb, **lay** takes a direct object, in this case, **assault rifles. Lie** is an intransitive verb meaning **recline** or **be located.** *The alligators lie in the ditch.*

lead, led

Lead is often used incorrectly as the past tense form of the verb, **lead,** possibly because it is pronounced the same as the word for the metal, **lead.** The proper past tense form is **led.** *The conversation led nowhere.*

leave, let

Leave should not be used to mean **allow.** It is inappropriate to say, *Leave us go to the store.* The proper term in this case is **let.**

lend, loan

Loan is a noun that is often used incorrectly instead of the verb, **lend.** In formal writing, it is mistaken to say, *We loaned them our fax machine.* The sentence should read, *We lent them our fax machine.*

less, fewer

See also FEWER, LESS.

let, leave

See also LEAVE, LET.

liable, likely, apt

See also APT, LIKELY, LIABLE.

lie, lay

See also LAY, LIE.

lightening, lightning

Lightening is the gerund form of the verb, **lighten.** *We felt the somber mood lightening.* **Lightning** is the electrical flash that accompanies thunderstorms.

like, as

See also AS, LIKE.

likely, liable, apt

See also APT, LIKELY, LIABLE.

likewise

Likewise is an adverb that is often misused as a conjunction. It is inappropriate to say, *I cleaned the valves, the rings, likewise the casings.* **Likewise** should be used to refer to the manner in which an event occurs. *I cleaned the valves and rings with solvent and a toothbrush. I cleaned the casings likewise.*

Linking verbs

Linking verbs relate the subject of a clause or sentence to the subject complement, identifying the subject and subject complement as equivalent. Linking verbs include **appear, be, become, grow, remain, seem,** and the sense verbs, **feel, look, smell, sound,** and **taste.** *We are satisfied. The water tastes musty. The weeds grow tall.*

See also SUBJECT and SUBJECT COMPLEMENTS.

Lists

Lists are series of like constructions. They may be related by a coordinating conjunction and separated by commas or semicolons. Each item in a list should take the same grammatical form. *I like swimming with my socks on, drinking scotch from a baby bottle, and speculating about the private lives of politicians.* In this list of things identifying what I like, each item is a gerund phrase. Items in a list may be separated by semicolons rather than commas when they are long clauses that might not otherwise seem like parts of a list. *You know the end is near when your neighbors sneak into your pool and swim with their socks on; when grown men drink expensive scotch out of baby bottles; and when the private lives of our elected officials are subject to the perverse imaginings of anarchists and deviants.*

See also **PARALLEL STRUCTURE.**

Literal language

Literal language means what it says, in contrast to figurative language, which means other than what it says. In all likelihood, the expression, **I had him eating out of my hand** may literally be applied only to animals being tamed. Figuratively, the expression may be applied to anyone who cooperates fully.

See also **FIGURATIVE LANGUAGE.**

literal, literate

Literal means **as written.** *Taken literally, the phrase, "take a hike" does not necessarily sound bad.* **Literate** means **familiar with written language.** *Literate people are often less gullible than others.*

livid

Livid is often used to mean reddened, but properly means pale. *The blood drained from her face, leaving her livid.*

loan, lend

See also **LEND, LOAN.**

loosen, unloosen

Loosen and **unloosen** are both used to mean **untie, disconnect,** or otherwise **make less tight,** but **unloosen** is colloquial and should be avoided in formal writing. Contrast **ravel** and **unravel,** both of which are acceptable in formal discourse.

See also RAVEL, UNRAVEL.

lot

See also A LOT, ALOT, ALLOT.

M

Main clauses
See also INDEPENDENT CLAUSES.

Main forms
The main forms of words are usually present tense verbs or singular nouns except where the noun or verb form requires a prefix or suffix. The main form of the adjective, **beautiful,** is the noun, **beauty.** The main form of the noun, **happiness,** is the adjective, **happy.**

See also COMBINING FORMS.

majority, plurality
Majority means **most of the total.** *The majority of cars use an internal combustion engine.* **Plurality** means **most of any subgroup.** *The plurality of the votes went to the democratic candidate, who received 30 percent of the total.*

Male pronoun
See also GENERIC HE.

mandatory, compulsory
See also COMPULSORY, MANDATORY.

Mass nouns

Mass nouns are people and things that cannot be counted, including collective nouns such as **group** and abstractions such as **happiness.** In general, they should be used with singular verb forms.

See also AMOUNT and COLLECTIVE NOUNS.

may be, maybe

May be is a verb phrase meaning **possibly is** or **possibly will be. Be** in this sense is the subjunctive mood form of the verb, **is,** and is necessary because **may** indicates a conditional situation. *The weather may be warm tomorrow. The casserole may be done by now.* **Maybe** is an adverb meaning **possibly** and is usually used as a sentence modifier. *Maybe it will rain.* **Maybe** is a casual term and should be avoided in formal writing.

See also CONDITIONAL SENTENCES and SUBJUNCTIVE MOOD.

may, can

See also CAN, MAY.

may, might

May and **might** are basically interchangeable verb forms meaning **have permission** or **be possible. May** differs from **might** in being more emphatic. Something that may happen is more likely than something that might happen. Something one may do is condoned more than something one might do. **Might** is the past tense form of **may** and should be used rather than **may** to express the past perfect tense. *The house might have caved in by now.* Both **might** and **may,** however, are used to express present and future tenses. Although **might** is properly a past tense form of **may, might** also serves as an optional subjunctive form. *The house might cave in tomorrow.*

See also SUBJUNCTIVE MOOD.

means

Means is a collective noun that may be used with either a singular or a plural pronoun or verb. When used as a synonym for resources it takes plural forms. *I have the means to take care of myself.* When used as a synonym for **way** it may take plural or singular forms. *A good means of getting what you want is asking for it. All means of getting things suit desperate people.*

See also COLLECTIVE NOUNS.

meantime, meanwhile

Meantime and **meanwhile** should not be used interchangeably. **Meantime** is a noun. *I'll be gone two hours; make good use of the meantime.* **Meanwhile,** is an adverb. *I'll be gone two hours; meanwhile you can clean the garage.*

media, medium

Media is the plural form of the word **medium.** *The artist works in many media. His best medium is clay.* Neither **medias** nor **mediums** is acceptable.

mediate, arbitrate

See also ARBITRATE, MEDIATE.

meretricious, meritorious

It is bad to be meretricious but good to be meritorious. **Meretricious** means **seemingly, or superficially good, but actually not good.** *The promise of warm hospitality on the invitation was meretricious; we were ignored and got nothing to eat.* **Meritorious** means **worthy** or **of merit.** *Too bad her performance in class is not as meritorious as on the playing field.*

Metaphor

Metaphor is the use of a concrete term to represent something other than the thing the term ordinarily stands for. *Whenever Gary thinks about his noodle business, his mind becomes a beehive.* Here **beehive** is a metaphor for Gary's mind. **Gary's mind** is what is known as the tenor of the metaphor, the metaphor's literal term; **beehive** is what is known as the vehicle, the metaphor's figurative term.

Metaphors can be useful for depicting ideas and situations vividly, but they should not be used unless they point to a clear, significant resemblance between tenor and vehicle. *When we finally arrived at the house, the porch light shone like a leaping gazelle.* Here there is no evident connection between the porch light and a leaping gazelle. The metaphor is therefore inappropriate.

In general, metaphors should be used with care. They often say more about a writer's desire to be creative than about the topic at hand. Trendy, commonplace metaphors such as, *We busted our humps* or *the sharks in the boardroom* have no place in serious writing.

See also CONCRETE LANGUAGE; FIGURATIVE LANGUAGE; and MIXED METAPHORS.

million, millions

Million may be used for more than one million when referring to a specific number. *Our company sold over three million widgets.* **Millions** may be used to refer to a number in the millions that is estimated or not specific. *Our company sold millions of widgets.*

minimum, minimal

Minimum is a noun; **minimal** is an adjective. *The enthusiasm of the class was minimal. There were a minimum of participants.*

Misplaced modifiers

Misplaced modifiers are phrases that occur in an inopportune place in a sentence, making the sentence less clear than it would otherwise be. In general, modifiers should stand as closely as possible to the words they modify. The following sentence contains misplaced modifiers: *I got a new job the day before yesterday with the city installing computers.* The modifiers, **with the city** and **installing computers** should be closer to **job,** the word they modify. The sentence should read, *The day before yesterday I got a new job with the city installing computers.*

See also **MODIFIERS.**

Mixed metaphors

Mixed metaphors result from the use of two different metaphors to illustrate a single idea or situation. They generally exhibit confusion on the writer's part and should be avoided, although they can be amusing. *The defendant's assertions were unvarnished tripe.* **Unvar-**

nished tripe is a mixed metaphor since it compares the defendant's assertions both to a material surface such as wood that can be varnished and to a kind of food.

mobile, movable

Mobile means **capable of motion** or **designed for movement.** *I'm designing a mobile bed so people can sleep on their way to work.* **Movable** means **capable of being moved.** It is distinct from **portable** in that movable things are generally not carried by a single person. *The filing cabinet was movable as it was, so we did not bother to empty it.*

Modal verbs

Modal verbs are helping verbs that express various degrees of inclination or ability. They include **can** and **could, may** and **might, must** and **ought, shall** and **should,** and **will** and **would.** *We should eat our casserole, but I would rather crawl on my hands and knees through a swamp.* Modal verbs take the same form regardless of whether the verb mood is declarative or subjunctive and regardless of the pronoun they are used with: *I ought, you ought, she ought, we ought, you ought.*

Modifiers

Modifiers are adjectives and adverbs as well as adjective clauses and adverb clauses, those groups of words that act as adjectives and adverbs. Modifiers further define or characterize nouns, verbs, pronouns, or other modifiers.

See also ADJECTIVES, ADVERBS, CLAUSES, DANGLING MODIFIERS, MISPLACED MODIFIERS, and SQUINTING MODIFIERS.

moneys
Moneys may be used to refer to more than one kind of currency. **Monies** should not be used.

monolithic, monumental
Monolithic and **monumental** have similar meanings but differing connotations. **Monolithic** is often used to characterize an erroneous conception of scope and coherence. *Morality is not monolithic, but requires negotiation.* **Monumental** is often used to describe something large, but not necessarily useful. *The activists made a monumental effort to change public opinion.*

Mood of verb
Verb moods indicate whether an action takes the form of a statement or question, a command, or a speculation. Unnecessary shifts in verb mood should be avoided. There are three verb moods: the indicative or declarative mood, the imperative mood, and the subjunctive mood.

The indicative mood makes a statement or asks a question. *Barnacles eat unceasingly. Are you certain?* Here, **eat** makes a statement and **are** asks a question.

The imperative mood issues a command. *Eat. Be gluttonous.* Here, **eat** and **be** issue commands.

The subjunctive mood expresses uncertainty or speculation. *If a barnacle stopped eating, it would have nothing to do.* Here, **would have** indicates that the situation is conditional.

See also CONDITIONAL SENTENCES; CONSISTENCY; DECLARATIVE MOOD; IMPERATIVE MOOD; and SUBJUNCTIVE MOOD.

moral, morale
Moral is an adjective that is used in reference to good and evil. *The decision to go to war is moral as well as tactical.* **Morale** is a noun meaning **good spirits** and **dignity.** *Morale at school went down when they stopped serving dessert.*

more with a verb
More is an indefinite pronoun that may take either a plural or a singular verb, depending on the noun referred to. When the noun to which **more** refers is a count noun, **more** should take a plural verb form. *More dirty diapers are on the way!* If the noun **more** refers to is a mass noun, a singular verb is required. *More dirty laundry is forthcoming!*

See also COLLECTIVE NOUNS, COUNT NOUNS, and IN-DEFINITE PRONOUNS.

more equal
See also EQUAL, MORE.

more important, importantly
See also IMPORTANT, IMPORTANTLY.

more than, better than
See also BETTER THAN, MORE THAN.

most, almost
Most is sometimes used improperly instead of **almost.** *They are most finished washing the car.* **Most** should be used to mean **as much as possible.** **Almost** should be used to mean **nearly.**

most and verb

Most is an indefinite pronoun which, like **more,** can take either a plural or a singular verb depending on the noun referred to.

See also **INDEFINITE PRONOUNS** and **MORE WITH A VERB.**

most, mostly

Both **most** and **mostly** may be used as adjectives. **Most** should be used to mean **most extremely.** *We are both at fault but you are most to blame.* **Mostly** may be used to mean **almost completely,** but its use should be reserved for casual speech and writing. In formal writing, use **nearly** or **almost.**

movable, mobile

See also **MOBILE, MOVABLE.**

much, muchly

Muchly is never correct. **Much** may be used as an adverb and as an adjective.

must, ought

Must and **ought** are modal verbs, which are special kinds of linking verbs. Thus, they ought not to be used with other linking verbs. It is a mistake to say, *They had ought to go to the fashion show.*

Ought should be used with infinitive verb forms, such as **to go** and **to think. Must** should not be used with infinitives.

Ought indicates a less urgent necessity than **must,** but a more urgent necessity than **should.**

See also **INFINITIVES** and **MODAL VERBS.**

mutual, common, shared

See also COMMON, MUTUAL, SHARED.

myself

Myself is a reflexive personal pronoun that is often misused as a substitute for I or **me** where no reflexive pronoun is required. It is acceptable to say, *I amaze myself,* since **myself** is used here reflexively. It is inappropriate, however, to say, *She amazes Clara and myself.* The proper term here is **me.** It is also incorrect to say, *Clara and myself are amazing.* The proper term here is **I.**

N

Narrative

Narrative is discourse presented in story form, relating events in sequential order. It contrasts with exposition, which explains ideas or advances an argument. Narrative features can often be found in expository writing just as expository elements can be found in most narrative.

nature

The word **nature** is often used in a meaningless way and could often be omitted. *The problem was of a perplexing nature*. Here the idea of **nature** contributes no information and should be left out. A clearer, more direct statement is, *The problem was perplexing*.

nauseous, nauseated

Nauseous properly means **causing nausea**. *Nauseous fumes emanated from her closet*. **Nauseated** properly means **sickened**. *I was nauseated by the ceremony*. **Nauseous**, however, is used so frequently to mean **nauseated** that the distinction has all but disappeared.

Necessary clauses and phrases

See also ESSENTIAL CLAUSES AND PHRASES.

necessity, need

Necessity and **need** mean the same thing but are used differently. **Need** may be used with infinitives, but **necessity** may only be used with **for** or **of.** *We need to diet. We have a necessity of eating less.*

Negatives

Negatives are words that negate other words. They may be pronouns such as **none,** adjectives such as **no, few,** or **less,** or adverbs such as **hardly, scarcely, never, rarely,** and **not.** The prefix **un-** also functions as a negative adverb, since it can be placed in front of verbs to negate them. Negatives also may be verbs such as **lack.**

Negative assertions should be avoided whenever positive statements would be clearer. *They have less peanut butter when the manager doesn't come to work.* This sentence could be revised to read, *They have more peanut butter when the manager comes to work.*

See also **DOUBLE NEGATIVES.**

neither, nor

Neither . . . nor is a paired correlative conjunction used to negate both of two opposed terms. When the terms are plural, they should take a plural verb form. *Neither peas nor carrots supply much vitamin C.* When **neither** is used to negate singular nouns, the verb should take the singular form. *Neither a frog nor a toad gives people warts.* When one term is singular and the other is plural, the verb takes the form of the term to which it is closest. *Neither the dog nor the cats are much help around the house.*

See also **EITHER, OR.**

Neologism

A neologism is a recently invented word such as **internet.** Some neologisms become part of standard English, but others do not.

nevertheless, never the less

Nevertheless is similar in meaning to **but,** but it makes a more emphatic contrast. It should be written as one word, not three.

noisome, noisy

Noisome is an adjective that refers not to sound, but to smell and means **offensive.** *The noisome odor of sulphur hung in the air all the time.* Noisome can also mean **generally offensive. Noisy** is an adjective or an adverb that refers to sound. It is sometimes used figuratively to refer to complex visual designs. *I don't like the pattern on that sofa; it is too noisy.*

Nominal forms

Nominal forms are nouns made from verbs or adjectives. **Sleepiness,** for example, is the nominal form of the adjective, **sleepy.**

Nonessential clauses and phrases

Nonessential clauses and phrases are word groups that can be omitted from a sentence without contradicting its meaning. Unlike essential clauses and phrases, nonessential elements should be separated from the rest of the sentence with commas. *The pangolin, whose fur is scaly, lives in Asia and Africa.*

Nonparallel structure

See also FAULTY PARALLELISM.

Nonrestrictive elements

See also NONESSENTIAL CLAUSES AND PHRASES.

Non sequitur

A Latin term meaning, **does not follow,** a non sequitur is a statement that has no evident relation to the statement that precedes it. *It is foggy today. My son's baseball team is doing well this season.*

Nonsexist terminlolgy

See also INCLUSIVE LANGUAGE.

none and verb

None is a negative indefinite pronoun that can take either a singular or plural verb depending on the noun it modifies. *None of us are night-wandering bloodsuckers.* Here, **none** refers to the plural noun, **bloodsuckers.** The verb, **are,** is therefore plural. *None of the bloodsucking has proven fatal.* Here, **none** refers to the singular noun, **bloodsucking.** The verb, **has proven,** is therefore singular.

See also INDEFINITE PRONOUNS.

nonetheless, none the less

Nonetheless, like **nevertheless,** is similar in meaning to **but,** but makes a more emphatic contrast. It should be written as one word rather than three.

Nonstandard usage

Nonstandard usage is the use of a term or phrase in a way that differs from the accepted practice of most other speakers and writers. *There are no dodo birds left anywheres in Australia.* Here **anywheres** is a nonstandard term for **anywhere.** Sometimes, nonstandard usage is a source of confusion, as when **neither** is used to mean **either** or when **irregardless** is used at all. Even when it is not confusing, however, nonstandard usage suggests to a writer's audience that he or she is unacquainted with accepted usage and may therefore be strange or inexperienced.

To be sure, tolerance for nonstandard usage has increased considerably in recent years. The failure to distinguish between **like** and **as**, or **imply** and **infer** is now common and often goes unnoticed even among professional speakers and writers. Punctilious diction, on the other hand, is as likely to offend as to impress. Many feel uncomfortable stating agreement by saying **surely,** as proper usage dictates, since **sure** sounds much more straightforward and affable.

In formal writing, however—notwithstanding any populist or provincial sympathies we may have—nonstandard usage must be eschewed. By observing standard rules of grammar and by using words with the exactness made possible by shared definitions and usages, we enable ourselves to write with greater clarity, accuracy, scope, and variety of conception. Although nonstandard usage may lend local color to formal writing and convey something of a writer's personality, a colloquial, familiar tone can be detrimental to effective communication. Therefore, although nonstandard usage is often fine in casual conversation, it should be eliminated from formal writing.

nor
See also NEITHER, NOR

not nearly, nowhere near
Nowhere near is sometimes used colloquially instead of **not nearly**. **Not nearly** is more acceptable in standard English.

notable, noted, notorious
Notable means worthy of being noticed, but it is usually used to refer to people and things who are already well-known. **Noted** means known and is used interchangeably with notable. **Notorious** means **infamous** or **well-known for reprehensible reasons.**

nothing
Where **nothing** is the subject of a sentence, it always takes a singular verb, even when it is qualified by a plural noun. *Nothing but the smallest ones is cast aside.*
See also INDEFINITE PRONOUNS.

Noun clauses
Noun clauses are dependent clauses that function as nouns. *Whatever hardships you face will make you a richer person.* Here, the noun clause, **whatever hardships you face,** is the subject of the verb, **will make.**

Noun determiners
See also DETERMINERS.

Noun phrases

Noun phrases are word groups made up of nouns, adjectives, and determiners that function as nouns in a sentence. Some noun phrases are **a greasy ball bearing, the third time this week,** and **a swig of Clorox.** Noun phrases, unlike noun clauses, do not contain their own predicates.

See also NOUN CLAUSES.

Noun-pronoun agreement

A singular pronoun requires a singular antecedent; a plural pronoun requires a plural antecedent. *A frog will rarely jump as far as it can.* Here, the singular noun, **frog,** takes the singular pronoun, **it.** *Frogs tend to be lazy unless they are swimming.* Here, the plural noun, **frogs,** takes the plural pronoun, **they.**

Traditionally, the male pronoun, **he,** has been used along with indefinite pronouns **everybody, everyone, somebody, someone,** etc., regardless of whether or not women were being referred to. *Everyone should love his country.* Recently, this has come to be considered biased or noninclusive language. Some alternatives are, *Everyone should love her country,* and *All people should love their country.*

See also CONSISTENCY and GENERIC HE.

Nouns

Nouns refer to persons, places, and things. They may be abstract or concrete, collective or numbered, common or proper, specific or general. Understanding differences in kinds of nouns can add clarity to one's writing and facilitate one's command of the rules of grammar.

Abstract nouns refer to things that cannot be directly perceived with any of the five senses, including **effervescence** and **ugliness.** Concrete nouns refer to things that can be sensed, such as **mist.**

Collective nouns refer to groups of things and people. Some collective nouns are **conglomeration** and **bevy.** Numbered, or count nouns refer to things that can be counted such as **salamander** and **television set.**

Common nouns refer to things that are not one of a kind. Some common nouns are **tea bag** and **oscillation.** Proper names, which are always capitalized, are names that refer to one-of-a kind people, places, and things such as the **New York Mets, Zanzibar,** and **George Clooney.**

General and specific are relative qualities of noun. **Dog** is a more specific, less general noun than **animal. Chihuahua** is a more specific noun than **dog.**

See also ABSTRACT LANGUAGE; CONCRETE LANGUAGE; COLLECTIVE NOUNS; COMMON NOUNS; COUNT NOUNS; GENERAL TERMS; PROPER NOUNS; and SPECIFIC TERMS.

number, amount

See also AMOUNT, NUMBER.

Numbered nouns

See also COUNT NOUNS.

numerous

Numerous, interchangeable with **many,** should not be used with a preposition. It is thus inappropriate to say *Numerous of the fish were guppies.* Instead, one should say, *There were numerous guppies among the other fish.*

O

Object case

English pronouns are inflected to take the subject case, the object case, or the possessive case. The object case identifies the pronoun as that which receives the action referred to by the verb. *We help them.* Here, **them** is the object of the verb, **help**; **we** is the subject. **Them** is the object case form of the pronoun whose subject case form is **they.** *They help us.* Here, **us** is the object and **they** is the subject.

The object usually appears after the verb, but sometimes precedes it, as in the question, *To whom do you owe a back rub?* Here, **whom,** the object, precedes the verb. Object pronouns that precede verbs are easily distinguished from subject pronouns because they require prepositions such as **to, for, at,** and **of.** The object case form, however, is often ignored in favor of the subject case form when the object precedes the verb. *Who are you waiting for?*

Just as the subject case form is often used for objects that precede the verb, the object case form is often mistakenly used for subjects that come after the verb. *I don't like cattle calls as much as him.* Here, the object case form, **him** is used inappropriately. The sentence should read, *I don't like cattle calls as much as he.*

See also CASE and PRONOUN CASES.

Object complements

Object complements are adjectives that modify objects.
Years of smoking have made the room dingy. Here,
dingy is the object complement and **room** is the object.

Objectivity

Traditionally considered a desirable attitude in expository writing, objectivity has been shown to be unattain-
able in any form of discourse having to do with human
beings. Thus it is acceptable and even desirable for writers to acknowledge and explain their positions as fully
as possible rather than pretend to neutrality regarding
issues that matter.

Objects

Objects are nouns and pronouns that receive rather than
produce the action referred to by a verb. *Birds eat insects.* Here, **insects** is the object of the verb, **eat.** Objects may be direct or indirect and may or may not take
prepositions.

Direct objects do not take prepositions. *I waxed the
floor.* Here **floor** is a direct object. Indirect objects may
take prepositions. *I waxed the floor for my health.* Here,
my health is an indirect object that takes the preposition, **for.**

See also DIRECT OBJECT; INDIRECT OBJECT; OBJECT
CASE; and PRONOUN CASES.

obliged, obligated

Obliged and **obligated** are similar, but **obligated,** unlike **obliged,** cannot be used to refer to feelings of gratitude. **Obliged** can be used to refer to gratitude and to

more forceful compulsion. *We are obliged to you for your help. We are obligated (or obliged) to serve on jury duty.*

observance, observation

An observance is a ceremonial practice. *Setting food on the shrine is an observance we practice daily.* An observation is something noticed. *It has been my observation that ignorant people are especially quick to criticize and slow to analyze.*

obsolescent, obsolete

Obsolescent and **obsolete** are similar in meaning, differing only in degree. **Obsolescent** may be used to refer to things that are in the process of becoming old-fashioned. *When you save money for a few years, you find that everything you own is obsolescent.* **Obsolete** means already out of date. *It doesn't take long for computer software to become obsolete.*

obviate, obvious

Obviate means **prevent**. *Her timely warning obviated a terrible accident.* **Obvious** means **readily apparent**. *His uncommon desire to please was obvious to everyone.*

occur, take place

Occur is an appropriate term for referring to a spontaneous, unplanned event. *An accident occurred.* **Take place** is appropriate for referring to an event that was planned or organized. *A rally took place.*

of

Of is a preposition that is often used unnecessarily as in the phrases, **alongside of, half of,** and **inside of. Of** should be omitted from these phrases.

of, have

See also COULD HAVE, OF.

off of

The preposition **of** is unnecessary in conjunction with the preposition **off.** It is thus incorrect to say, *Get off of my Fabergé egg.* This sentence should read, *Get off my Fabergé egg.*

oh, O

Oh and **O** have differing uses. **Oh** may stand as an exclamation by itself, or be used with other exclamations, as in **oh, shoot!** **O** is properly used as a form of address as in **O ye gods of semantic propriety! O** is always capitalized. **Oh** is only capitalized when it begins a sentence.

okay, ok, O.K., OK

These terms are unacceptable in formal writing. The word **satisfactory** is the best formal alternative. In informal writing, all of these forms, as well as others, including **oke-doke,** denote a satisfactory state of affairs.

old adage

The phrase **old adage** is redundant since **adage** means **old saying.**

older, elder
See also ELDER, OLDER.

on account of
On account of is often used colloquially instead of **because. Because** is preferable in formal writing.

on behalf of, in behalf of
See also BEHALF.

on to, onto
On to should be used when **on** is an adverb modifying a continued action. *The scooter rolled on, to the delight of the crowd.* **Onto** should be used as a single preposition. *The mice had jumped up onto the table.*

only
When used as an adverb, **only** should be placed after the verb it modifies in order to avoid ambiguity. The following sentence should be rewritten: *They not only began the process of restructuring the company, but hiring new personnel.* This sentence should read, *They began the processes not only of restructuring the company, but of hiring new personnel.*

oppress, repress, suppress
Oppress, repress, and **suppress** all mean **restrain,** but should be used to refer to different things. **Suppress** is the most general of these terms. It may be used to refer to desires, actions, and people. When used to refer to people, it suggests that there is a specific characteristic or action being restrained. *I was suppressed in my history class because I talk too much. I had to suppress the*

urge to object. **Oppress** refers exclusively to people. It often refers in general to hardships inflicted on one group of people by another. It may also refer to a specific hardship suffered by a specific person. *The powerful oppress the weak. I am oppressed by a stone in my shoe.* **Repress** resembles **suppress** except that it is often used to refer specifically to feelings and desires. Thus someone who is repressed does not know how to express their feelings properly. *Some men repress the desire to communicate because it makes them feel vulnerable.*

or
When **or** is used as a conjunction between singular nouns, the verb should be singular as well. *A screwdriver, a pocketknife, or a chisel is more useful than a fingernail.* When **or** relates singular and plural nouns, the verb should agree with the noun nearest to it. *You or your friends are expected tomorrow. They or I will finish the work then.*

oral, verbal, aural
Oral means **spoken.** *We have an oral agreement.* **Verbal** may mean either **written** or **spoken.** *They have excellent verbal skills.* Frequently, however, **verbal** is used to mean **spoken** rather than written. *We have a verbal agreement.* Such usage of **verbal** may be ambiguous. One should not say, *I need verbal notification by tomorrow,* if one requires word-of-mouth information. **Aural** pertains to the sense of hearing. *His aural faculties were diminishing.*

Order of words

Because English is not highly inflected, the order of words is often an important indication of the different parts of speech. *We ate octopi,* has a different meaning from *Octopi ate us.* In the first example **we** is the subject and **octopi** is the object. Subject and object are reversed with word order in the second example.

orientate

Orientate is a nonstandard term used in place of **orient** and should be avoided.

Originality

Originality is the desirable quality of all analytic writing. It is achieved not by being quirky or stylish but by showing how one's ideas contribute to a body of ideas already in place and by making those ideas recognizable to readers. A piece of writing that simply makes assertions no one has made before is not necessarily original; it may be nonsensical instead. Unprecedented assertions avoid seeming nonsensical when they are related to other, familiar assertions as either further applications of old ideas or as additions or corrections.

See also **ATTRIBUTION** and **CONTEXT**.

Ought, must

See also **MUST, OUGHT**.

overexaggerate

The addition of the word **over** to **exaggerate** is redundant, since **exaggerate** already suggests excess and is sufficient by itself. **Over** should be omitted.

overly

Overly may be used in casual speech as a synonym for **excessively.** In formal writing, however, it should be avoided. It is more precise to make a compound word out of **over** and the term it modifies as in **overeager** or **overtired.**

P

Paragraphs

Paragraphs are sections of writing that develop an idea. They may be as short as a single sentence or as long as a page or two, but they generally range from three to ten sentences in length. Paragraphs, however, ought not be divided arbitrarily by length, but should present an idea in relation to previous ideas and move from a general to a particular account of the idea. However many sentences it takes to explain the idea fully is the proper length for a paragraph. If the paragraph grows too long to be easily understood as the explication of a single idea, it should be divided into smaller paragraphs, each dealing with a separate and more specific aspect of the original larger paragraph.

Parallel structure

All words, phrases, and clauses should have the same grammatical structure as other words, phrases, and clauses to which they are joined by a coordinating conjunction such as **and, but, or,** and so.

See also FAULTY PARALLELISM and LISTS.

parameter

Parameter is often used imprecisely to mean **boundary** or **limit.** *By smoking a second cigarette you ex-*

ceeded the parameters of our agreement. Many readers disapprove of such usage and prefer to see **parameter** restricted to its mathematical sense.

Paraphrase

A paraphrase is the conversion of a piece of writing into new words. For example, the sentence, *There are too many people at the beach,* may be paraphrased, *The shore is too crowded.* When using another's work without directly quoting it, that work should be paraphrased and the author acknowledged, unless the paraphrased material is common knowledge. Failure to acknowledge the source of another's original work in one's own writing is plagiarism, which is punishable by law. Although paraphrasing another's work makes quotation marks unnecessary, it does not exempt one from having to cite the source of the paraphrase.

See also CITATION and QUOTATIONS.

Parentheses

Parentheses are punctuation marks used to separate nonessential words from the rest of a sentence. *All the doughnuts (most of them were jelly-filled) had been crammed into holes in the wall.* Parentheses should be used for elements that do not require much emphasis. Commas may be used to set off words that require more emphasis, or dashes for even greater emphasis.

When a parenthesis concludes a sentence, the period should be placed after it. *The holes in the wall had been crammed full of doughnuts (most of them jelly-filled).* Commas should not be used together with parentheses.

Parenthetical elements

Parenthetical elements are words and word groups that are not essential to the meaning of a sentence and are separated from it by means of parentheses, commas, or dashes. *The animal rights activist—wearing patent leather shoes—spoke passionately for twenty minutes.*

partially, partly

Partially may be used to refer to things that are not complete in themselves and to conditions that are not extreme. *The keg is partially full.* **Partly** may be used to refer to things that share characteristics with other things. *The lake is partly on our property.* **Partly to blame** means **sharing blame. Partially to blame** means **not entirely at fault.**

Participial phrases

Participial phrases are word groups beginning with participles that function as adjectives or adverbs. *I emerged from the ocean holding a live fish between my teeth.* Here the participial phrase, **holding a live fish between my teeth,** serves as an adjective modifying the subject, **I.**

Participles

Participles are verb forms that, together with helping verbs, make up part of the whole verb. Participles may also serve as adjectives or adverbs. The two kinds of participles are present participles and past participles. Present participles are formed by adding **-ing** to the main form of the verb. The present participle is also known as the gerund form of the verb. *I am hoping there*

will be some dirt left in the garden after the tornado.
Here, **hoping** is a present participle serving as a verb together with the helping verb, **am.**

Past participles are formed in any of a number of
ways, most commonly by adding -**ed** to the end of the
main form of the verb. *Selected at random for kitchen
detail, Private Hendricks spit in the soup.* Here, **selected** is a past participle used as part of the adjective
clause, **selected at random.** Other past participles are
blown, felt, kept, and **swum.**

Past participles sometimes take the same form as the
past tense of a verb, such as **felt** and **kept.** Often, however, the past participle, such as **blown** or **swum,** is different from the past tense form, **blew** or **swam.**

Past participles sometimes differ in certain regions
from standard English. In formal writing, such variants
are unacceptable.

Incorrect Past Participles
*I had . . . thinked, thunk, saw, seed, drove, catched, bit,
hid, clumb, swang, growed, flang, flinged, wishted,
eated, eat, heared, etc.*

See also **GERUNDS.**

Particles
Particles are prepositions that accompany verbs and influence their meanings. *It was nice of you to come over
now that this problem has come up.* Here **over** and **up**
are particles. Some other particles are **away, back,
down, in, of, off, on, out, over, up,** and **with.**

See also **PREPOSITIONS.**

Parts of a sentence

See also **SENTENCES**.

Parts of speech

The parts of speech are nouns, pronouns, verbs, adjectives, adverbs, conjunctions, prepositions, and interjections. These different parts indicate differences in the function and meaning of words. Understanding differences among the various parts of speech is useful for understanding the rules of grammar.

party, person

Party may be used to refer to a group of people even though the group may or may not consist of a single individual. **Party,** however, should not be used to refer to an individual who is known to be an individual. In this case, **person** is the appropriate term.

Passive voice

In passive voice, as opposed to active voice, the subject of the sentence receives, rather than carries out, the action described by the verb. Verbs in passive voice are combined with a form of the verb, **be** to indicate that the subject receives the action. *We were amazed by the moths.* Here, the subject, **we** receives the action, **were amazed** perpetrated by the object, **moth.** The sentence restated in active voice reads, *The moths amazed us.*

In general, the active voice is preferable to the passive, since it presents action more directly. The passive voice, however, can be effective when it is desirable to emphasize the reception of an action rather than the agent.

Passive Voice Constructions
We were assisted by the police. The dogs were eaten alive by their fleas. I am pleased by your recovery. The checks were canceled.

See also **ACTIVE VOICE.**

Past participles
See also **PARTICIPLES.**

Past perfect progressive tense
The past perfect progressive tense indicates an action that began in the past and has continued, but which may or may not continue in the present. It is formed by using **had been** as a helping verb and adding **-ing** to the main form of the main verb. *The house had been crumbling for decades.*

See also **PERFECT TENSES** and **PROGRESSIVE TENSES.**

Past perfect tense
The past perfect tense indicates an action that began in the past and was completed before a later time in the past. It is formed by using **had** as a helping verb and adding **-ed** to the main verb form. *The birds had nested by the time we arrived.*

See also **PERFECT TENSES.**

Past progressive tense
The past progressive tense indicates a continuous action that occurred in the past. It is formed by using **was** as a helping verb and adding **-ing** to the main verb form. *I was wondering about blisters.*

See also **PROGRESSIVE TENSES.**

Past tenses

Past tenses indicate an action that took place in the past. The different past tenses are past perfect progressive, past perfect, past progressive, and simple past.

peaceable, peaceful

Peaceable refers to people or animals and means **willing to get along in peace.** *Kangaroos are generally peaceable.* **Peaceful** is a more general term meaning **quiet** and **undisturbed.** *There are too many kangaroos in my backyard for it to be peaceful.*

pedantic, pedagogical

Pedantic refers to the display of useless knowledge. *His formal manner seemed pedantic rather than penetrating.* **Pedagogical** refers to teaching and instruction. *Socratic method remains a popular pedagogical technique.*

people, peoples, persons

People, the plural of **person,** may be used to refer to more than one person. **Peoples,** the plural of **people,** may be used to refer to more than one cultural group. *The history of Western civilization records the actions of many peoples.*

In general, **people** should be used instead of **persons** as the plural of **person.** The exception to this rule is when specific people are referred to. *A group of four persons stood by the road.* In this case, either **persons** or **people** is acceptable.

Perfect tenses

Perfect tenses indicate actions completed before a reference point in time that they designate. The perfect tenses are past perfect, *We had spoken;* present perfect, *We have spoken;* and future perfect, *We will have spoken.*

perigee, apogee

See also APOGEE, PERIGEE.

Periods

Periods (.) are punctuation marks that indicate a sentence has ended. They are also used for abbreviations such as **Dr.** and B.C.

Periods belong inside quotation marks whenever they appear at the end of a sentence. *We said, "Aaaaah."* If parenthetical citations appear after a quotation, the period follows the final parenthesis. *Lady Macbeth says, "O, O, O!" (Act V, scene I).*

persecute, prosecute

Persecute means **bother continually.** *My cat persecutes the birds.* **Prosecute** means **press legal charges against.** *The state prosecutes an increasing number of drunk drivers every year.*

Person

Person refers to whether or not the speaker or writer or audience is the subject of discourse. There are three persons: first, second, and third. These forms are indicated by pronouns and verbs. First person pronouns are **I** and **we.** The second person pronoun is **you.** Third person pronouns are **he, she, it,** and **they.** Verb forms change to correspond with the different person forms.

See also FIRST PERSON, SECOND PERSON, and THIRD PERSON.

person, party
See also PARTY, PERSON.

Personal pronouns
Personal pronouns are pronouns that stand for people and things. The personal pronouns in the subject case are **I, you, she, he, it, we,** and **you.** In addition to the subject case, personal pronouns take the object case and the possessive case. Personal pronouns must agree in case, gender, and number with the nouns they refer to, known as their antecedents, and with the verbs that are their predicates. Personal pronouns in the object case may be reflexive if they take the same antecedent as the subject. *I hurt myself.* Here, **myself** is a reflexive personal pronoun.

See also AGREEMENT; ANTECEDENTS; PRONOUN CASES; and REFLEXIVE PRONOUNS.

persons, people
See also PEOPLE, PEOPLES, PERSONS.

perspective, prospective
Perspective is a noun meaning **point of view.** *Only someone with a jaundiced perspective would think doctors don't care about their patients' health.* **Prospective** is an adjective meaning **under consideration.** *All prospective employees should report to the lab for testing.*

phenomena, phenomenon

Phenomena is the plural of **phenomenon.** *Of all psychic phenomena, dreams are among the most instructive. No other phenomenon is as common, subconscious, and detectable.*

Phrases

A phrase, unlike a clause, does not have its own subject and predicate. Phrases are groups of related words that may function as nouns, verbs, adjectives, or adverbs. Different kinds of phrases are absolute, appositive, gerund, infinitive, and participial. Phrases may be essential or nonessential to the meaning of the sentence.

See also ABSOLUTE PHRASES; APPOSITIVES; DANGLING MODIFIERS; ESSENTIAL CLAUSES AND PHRASES; GERUND PHRASES; INFINITIVES; NONESSENTIAL CLAUSES AND PHRASES; NOUN PHRASES; PARTICIPIAL PHRASES; and VERBAL PHRASES.

piteous, pitiful

Piteous means **worthy of compassion.** *The field hospital was a piteous sight after the battle.* **Pitiful** means worthy of contempt. *He gave up after a pitiful attempt.*

Place names

Place names, which are proper nouns, should be capitalized. Terms for kinds of places should not be capitalized as they are common nouns. *Central Park is a large, urban park.* Because **Central Park** is the name of a particular place, it is capitalized, unlike the word **park,** which is used to mean a kind of place.

Plagiarism

Plagiarism is the crime, punishable by law, of using another writer's words, ideas, or format without assigning appropriate credit. The minimum credit necessary for a source is the author's name. It is often appropriate to include the title of the work, publication date, publisher, city of publication, and page numbers as well. If a source's words are used, they should be set off with quotation marks, (" "). If a source's ideas are used but are presented in different words, quotation marks should not be used, but the source should be cited nonetheless.

Information that is generally known does not need to be cited.

See also CITATION; PARAPHRASE; QUOTATIONS.

Plain verb form

The plain verb form is the present tense, first person form of the verb, or the infinitive form without **to.** It is this form that is generally used in dictionary entries.

plan ahead

The phrase **plan ahead** is redundant, since planning necessarily entails foresight. Thus it is preferable to say, *Let's plan the party* rather than, *Let's plan ahead for the party.*

See also REDUNDANCY.

plan on, to

The preposition, **on** and a gerund are often used casually with **plan.** *I plan on giving up.* In formal writing,

plan is properly followed by an infinitive. *I plan to give up*.

See also GERUNDS and INFINITIVES.

playwright, playwrite

The author of a play is properly referred to as a **playwright. Wright** is a term designating a craftsman who fashions things. **Playwrite** is a misspelling based on the association of dramatic composition with writing rather than with fashioning.

plurality, majority

See also MAJORITY, PLURALITY.

Plurals

Plurals are word forms that indicate more than one subject or object. Nouns and pronouns may be plural and take verbs in the plural form. Adjectives and adverbs are not inflected for number and do not take a plural form. The plural form of most nouns can be made by adding an **s** onto the end of the word, although there are many exceptions to this rule. Verbs are inflected to correspond to plural subjects and pronouns are inflected to correspond to plural antecedents.

plus

Plus is properly used as a preposition meaning **added to** or **in addition to**. *The sewage plus the burning tires made a horrible smell.*

Plus is often used colloquially as a conjunction meaning **moreover** or **furthermore**. Use of **plus** in this way is casual and should be avoided in formal discourse.

Chickens are smelly; plus they can be noisy in the morning.

politics

Politics, like many other words ending in **-ics,** may be considered a singular noun when it refers to an art or study. In such cases it requires a singular verb. *Politics is always a slippery business.* **Politics** is plural when it is used more specifically, as after **the, these, some** or a possessive noun or pronoun. *My politics are above suspicion.*

See also -ICS.

Positive form

Positive form is one of three forms of adjectives and adverbs including comparative form and superlative form. The positive form asserts a quality without assessing its degree in relation to other things that possess it: *The blue water rested peacefully.* Here, the adjective, **blue,** and the adverb, **peacefully,** take the positive form. Contrast the comparative forms of the same words: **bluer, more peacefully,** and the superlative form: **bluest, most peacefully.**

See also **ADJECTIVES, ADVERBS; COMPARATIVE FORM; COMPARISON;** and **SUPERLATIVE FORM.**

Possessive case

The possessive case is one of the three cases of nouns and pronouns in English including the subject case and the object case. Possessive case indicates that a thing owns or exhibits another thing or quality. Possessive case may also be used to indicate that an event happened to someone or something, as in **the rat's downfall** or **the**

mail carrier's arrival. Failure to use the possessive case in this way often results in fused participles. The possessive case of nouns is formed by adding **'s** to the main form of the noun. *Those are my dog's fleas.* Here **dog's** is the possessive case of the noun, **dog.**

None of the pronouns require an apostrophe (**'**) to form the possessive case. The possessive case pronouns are **my** and **mine, your** and **yours, her** and **hers, his, its, ours,** and **theirs.** *These mistakes are yours.* Here, **yours** is the possessive case of the pronoun, **you.**

Possessive case nouns are redundant when used after the phrases, **that of, those of,** and **these of.** Thus it is incorrect to say *Your hair resembles that of a dog's.* **Dog** should be used here instead of **dog's.** When personal pronouns are used after **that of, those of,** or **these of,** however, they take the possessive case. Thus one should say *Your freckles are smaller than these of mine* rather than **these of me.**

To form possessives of plural nouns ending in **s,** simply place an apostrophe after the plural word: **the flowers' aroma.** To form possessives of plural nouns not ending in **s,** add **'s** to the end of the word: **the nuclei's disintegration.**

Incorrect Possessives
*These are **your's**. It can't find **it's** home. This food is **their's**. The fault is all **our's**. My yard is as green as that of my **neighbor's**. It is the **childrens'** hour.*

Correct Possessives
These are yours. It can't find its home. This food is theirs. The fault is all ours. My yard is as green as that of my neighbor. It is the children's hour.

See also **FUSED PARTICIPLES.**

Possessive pronouns
See also **POSSESSIVE CASE**.

Postpositive adjective
A postpositive adjective is one such as **galore** or **akimbo** that properly occurs after the noun it modifies. *They lay in a heap at the bottom of the stairs, arms and legs akimbo.*

practicable, practical
Practicable means **feasible. Practical** has the further meaning of **prudent.** *It seems practicable, but not practical, to open a pizza parlor in the middle of nowhere.*

practically, virtually
Practically is often used colloquially to mean **in effect** or **for all intents and purposes. Virtually** is a preferred term in formal writing. *The twins are virtually indistinguishable.* Use of **practically** to mean **almost** should also be avoided.

precede, proceed
Precede is a verb meaning **appear before.** *My nose precedes me unless I walk backwards.* **Proceed** is a verb meaning **continue.** *After pausing to wipe his eyes, the prisoner proceeds to break stones.*

precipitant, precipitate, precipitous
As adjectives, these words have similar meanings. **Precipitate** and **precipitant** mean **rushing forward or falling suddenly.** They may be used to describe hasty human actions, physical things, or abstract movement. *My nasty letter elicited a precipitant response.* **Precipi-**

tous is chiefly used to refer to physical steepness. *We chose not to climb the precipitous incline.*

Precision

Precision is the desirable quality of formal discourse containing (1) words whose specific meanings are exactly used and (2) grammatical structures that present their meanings clearly. Imprecision results from words that merely approximate or even misrepresent the sense intended by their author and from grammatical constructions that fail to place emphasis where it belongs.

See also **FORMALITY**.

Predicate

The predicate is that part of a sentence that defines the action of the subject. It includes a verb and may also include direct objects, indirect objects, subject complements, and object complements.

Faulty predication occurs when the predicate indicates an action that is not carried out by the subject.

See also **FAULTY PREDICATION**.

Predicate adjectives

Also known as subject complements, predicate adjectives are related to the subject of a sentence by linking verbs. *You smell funny.* Here, **funny** is a predicate adjective modifying the subject **you**.

See also **LINKING VERBS** and **SUBJECT COMPLEMENTS**.

Predication, faulty

See also **FAULTY PREDICATION**.

Prefixes

Prefixes are combining forms that appear at the beginning of a word. Some prefixes are **anti-, dis-, pre-,** and **un-.** Some prefixes should be joined to words by means of a hyphen, although most do not require hyphenation. Prefixes that should usually be hyphenated are **all-, self-,** and **ex-,** when **ex-** means **erstwhile.**

See also HYPHENS.

prejudice, prejudiced

Prejudice is a noun meaning premature judgment. It is frequently used to refer to sexism, racism, or other social bias. *Her prejudice against men did not get in the way of her feelings for her bowling instructor.*

Prejudice is often mistakenly used as an adjective. It is incorrect to say, *They were prejudice against bald people.* Since **prejudice** is a noun, it requires the past participle form, **prejudiced,** if it is to function as an adjective, as in *prejudiced opinions,* or as part of a verb along with a helping verb as in *They were prejudiced.*

premiere, premier

Premiere, meaning a first performance, should not be used as a verb in formal writing. It is unacceptable to say, *The show premiered yesterday.* The proper term here is **opened. Premiere,** should not be confused with the word **premier,** which means first in rank.

Preparatory to, before

See also BEFORE, PREPARATORY TO.

Prepositional phrases

Prepositional phrases consist of prepositions such as **at, for, to,** and **with,** and the parts of a sentence known as objects. They typically function as adjectives or as adverbs. *I enjoy dancing with trained seals.* Here the prepositional phrase, **with trained seals,** modifies the verb, **enjoy dancing,** and thus functions as an adverb. *Some have the grace of professional dancers.* Here the prepositional phrase, **of professional dancers,** modifies the noun, **grace,** and thus functions as an adjective.

See also **PREPOSITIONS.**

Prepositions

Prepositions are words such as **at, for, to,** and **with** that relate transitive verbs to their objects. *I spoke to her.* Prepositions are often idiomatic, meaning that their use depends on acceptation rather than on a logical or grammatical rule. Thus proper prepositions must be learned by memory.

Some grammarians have asserted a preference for placing the preposition immediately before the object. *With whom are you going to the cattle call?* Most readers agree, however, that the preposition may appear at the end of a sentence in questions beginning with an object. *Whom are you going to the cattle call with?*

See also **IDIOMS, OBJECT CASE.**

prerequisite

The preposition **for** should not be used after **prerequisite.** When **prerequisite** is used as a noun, the proper preposition to use is **of.** *Hard work is a prerequisite of success.* When used as an adjective, **prerequisite** takes the proposition, **to.** *Hard work is prerequisite to success.*

prescribe, proscribe

Prescribe means recommend in written form. *Her letter prescribed avoiding Sigmund as much as possible.* **Proscribe** means **forbid the use of.** Common courtesy proscribes interrupting someone who is speaking.

Present participle

The present participle is a present tense verb form that can serve as an adjective or adverb or as a verb in combination with a helping verb. It is formed by adding **-ing** to the end of a main verb form. The present participle of the verb **climb** is **climbing.** The present participle is also known as the gerund form of the verb.

See also **PARTICIPLES.**

Present perfect progressive tense

Present perfect progressive tense indicates an action that begins in the past, continues in the present, and may continue into the future. It is made by using the past participle **has been** as a helping verb and adding the present participle **-ing** to the main form of the main verb. *The hamsters have been sleeping all day.*

See also **PERFECT TENSES** and **PROGRESSIVE TENSES.**

Present perfect tense

The present perfect tense indicates actions that begin in the past and may continue in the present. It is made by using **has** or **have** as a helping verb and adding it to the past participle form of the main verb. *We have eaten oysters.*

See also **PERFECT TENSES.**

Present progressive tense

The present progressive tense indicates an action that continues in the present. It is formed by using a form of the verb **be** as a helping verb added to the present participle of the main verb. *I am thinking of turpentine.*

See also PRESENT PARTICIPLE and PROGRESSIVE TENSES.

Present tenses

The present tenses are simple present, present progressive, present perfect, and present perfect progressive. These tenses indicate actions that take place or may take place in the present, including assertions of general truth.

See also PRESENT PERFECT PROGRESSIVE TENSE; PRESENT PERFECT TENSE; PRESENT PROGRESSIVE TENSE; and SIMPLE PRESENT TENSE.

presume, assume

See also ASSUME, PRESUME.

presumptive, presumptuous

Presumptive means **based on belief.** *The presumptive burglar turned out to be a porcupine.* **Presumptuous** means **overconfident.** *It was presumptuous of you to think you could watch the game on our TV set.*

pretense, pretext

Pretense means **deliberate falsehood.** *They made a pretense of being rich.* **Pretext** is similar in meaning to **pretense** but refers specifically to a pretended reason or excuse. *He remained behind to hear their conversation on the pretext of watering the plants.*

Preterit

Preterit or **preterite** applies to any past tense verb or to the past tenses in general.

prevent, avoid, avert

See also AVERT, AVOID, PREVENT.

prima facie, a priori

See also A PRIORI, PRIMA FACIE.

principal, principle

Principal and **principle** are often confused with one another. **Principal** is usually used as an adjective meaning **of primary importance.** It is also used as a noun as the title of a school official and as a financial term meaning **capital. Principle** is a noun meaning **rule, assumption, or truth.**

proceed, precede

See also PRECEDE, PROCEED.

Progressive tenses

The progressive tenses indicate continuing, uncompleted action. They are the present progressive, the present perfect progressive, the past progressive, the past perfect progressive, the future progressive, and the future perfect progressive. All the progressive tenses use helping verbs, including **is, has been, was, had been, will be,** and **will have been** in addition to the present participle **-ing** form of the main verb.

See also **PARTICIPLES.**

Pronoun cases

The three pronoun cases are the subject case, the object case, and the possessive case. The cases indicate the relation of personal pronouns to the verb. They also indicate possession. The subject case is used for pronouns that carry out the action indicated by the predicate. *We swim.* Here **we** is a subject case pronoun. The subject case pronouns are **I, you, she, he, it, we,** and **they.**

The object case is used for pronouns that receive the action indicated by the verb. *The water made us wet.* Here, **us** is an object case pronoun. The object case pronouns are **me, you, her, him, it, us,** and **them.**

The possessive case is used to show the association of a pronoun and something that pertains to it. There are different possessive pronouns for subject and object pronouns. *Our water is warm. The water is ours.* Here **our** is a subject case possessive pronoun; **ours** is an object case possessive pronoun. The possessive case subject pronouns are **my, your, her, his, its, our,** and **their.** The possessive case object pronouns are **mine, yours, hers, his, its, ours,** and **theirs.**

See also CASE and PERSONAL PRONOUNS.

Pronoun reference

All pronouns have an antecedent to which they refer, whether or not the antecedent is mentioned specifically. The antecedent of **I** is the person speaking or writing. The antecedent of **you** is the person being addressed.

Vague pronoun reference is a common problem in writing resulting from an unclear relationship between pronoun and antecedent. *When industries dump waste into our rivers, the polluted water kills plants, causing erosion and further damage to the environment. This has been identified as our most far-reaching environmental problem.* Here it is unclear to what the pronoun, **this** refers. The problem in question needs to be identified more specifically. Pronouns often used vaguely are **this** and **it**.

See also **PRONOUNS**.

Pronouns

Pronouns are parts of speech that stand for nouns. Pronouns may be personal, demonstrative, relative, interrogative, and indefinite. Personal pronouns stand for people and things. Some personal pronouns are **I, you, it, we,** and **they.** Personal pronouns may or may not be reflexive. Some reflexive pronouns are **myself, herself,** and **themselves.** Personal pronouns take different case forms. They may take the subject case, the object case, or the possessive case.

Demonstrative pronouns stand for things and indicate their conceptual or spatial immediacy. The demonstrative pronouns are **this, that, these,** and **those.** Demonstrative pronouns should not be inflected for possession as in **those's.**

Relative pronouns establish a relationship between nouns and dependent clauses that modify them. *I have a job that pays good money.* Here, **that** is a relative pronoun linking **job** with **pays good money.** The relative pronouns are **that, which, who, whom,** and **whose.**

Interrogative pronouns are relative pronouns used as questions. In effect, they relate the question to the noun that provides the answer. *What pays good money?*

Indefinite pronouns are pronouns that refer to non-specific antecedents. Some indefinite pronouns are **any-one, everybody, someone, either,** and **nothing.** Indefi-nite pronouns should be inflected for possession unless they end in **one** or **body,** as in **someone's.**

Pronouns must agree in form with their antecedents in terms of number and sometimes gender and with verbs in terms of person. Personal pronouns are also in-flected according to case to show their function relative to the action described by the verb.

See also AGREEMENT; DEMONSTRATIVE PRONOUNS; INDEFINITE PRONOUNS; PERSONAL PRONOUNS; POSSES-SIVE CASE; and PRONOUN CASES.

Proper nouns
Proper nouns are names for one-of-a-kind people, places, and things such as **Ed Garcia, Switzerland,** and the **Statue of Liberty.** They should be capitalized.

prophecy, prophesy
Prophecy is a noun meaning **prediction.** *His going bald was foretold in a prophecy.* **Prophesy** is a verb meaning **predict.** *We prophesied that he would go bald.*

proportional, proportionate
Proportional may be used to refer to the relationship of more than two related elements. *The quantities in each container are proportional to the others.* **Proportionate** may be used to refer to the relationship between two things. *The flour and baking soda are proportionate in each recipe.*

proscribe, prescribe
See also PRESCRIBE, PROSCRIBE.

prosecute, persecute
See also PERSECUTE, PROSECUTE.

prospective, perspective
See also PERSPECTIVE, PROSPECTIVE.

protagonist, antagonist
See also ANTAGONIST, PROTAGONIST.

provided, providing
When used as a conjunction to express a condition, **provided** should be used rather than **providing**. *We should have a good crop, provided that we get enough rain.*

proximity
See also CLOSE PROXIMITY.

punctilious, punctual
Punctilious means **taking great care with matters of etiquette.** It is often used in a mildly derogatory sense. *Her handshakes seemed more punctilious than warm.* **Punctual** means **on time.** *Few party guests are punctilious about being punctual.*

Punctuation
Punctuation consists of the marks used in writing other than letters, symbols, and numbers. These marks are periods, commas, question marks, exclamation points, colons, semicolons, ellipses, dashes, parentheses, quotation marks, apostrophes, underlines, hyphens, slashes, and brackets. Punctuation is mainly used for dividing words into understandable groups to enhance clarity

and to apportion emphasis, although some marks have other uses as well.

purposefully, purposely
Purposefully means **in order to achieve a desired result** and is usually used to refer to the manner in which something is done. *As he was introduced, he repeated each person's name purposefully, so they would know he was trying to remember them.* **Purposely** means **deliberately.** *The angry child spilled her milk purposely.*

Q

quandary, dilemma

See also DILEMMA, QUANDARY.

Question marks

Question marks (**?**) are end punctuation marks used
after direct questions.

Quotation marks

Quotation marks are marks of punctuation used for separating direct quotations from the rest of a text. *I feel
about modern dance much as Marianne Moore felt
about modern poetry: "I too dislike it."* Quotation
marks should only be used with quotations that are less
than three lines long. Otherwise, quotations should be
set off from the rest of the text in a hung paragraph.

Quotation marks are also used to indicate the title of
an article, essay, song, or short story: **"How to Avoid
Bad Things."** Underlines or italics should be used for
the titles of books, plays, and films.

Quotation marks may also be used instead of the
modifier **so-called** to indicate that a word or phrase
should be regarded critically. *We have all heard about
"overworked" managers.*

See also HUNG PARAGRAPHS and QUOTATIONS.

Quotations

Quotations are the use of one person's words by another person. They should be separated by quotation marks or in an indented, hung paragraph. Hung paragraphs are blocks of quoted text with wider margins than the non-quoted text. They should be used for quotations that exceed three lines. See also **Hung paragraph.**

Quotations should appear in a text as complete sentences or parts of complete sentences. If, for example, a writer quotes only the subject of another's sentence, he or she should provide the predicate in her or his own words. *Polonius admonishes Laertes to become neither "a borrower nor a lender" (Hamlet I, iii, 75).* The source of a quotation should be documented, either parenthetically as in the preceding example, or in a footnote or endnote. For parenthetical citations, the period follows the parenthesis. Otherwise, periods and commas should be placed inside the quotation marks. *"A borrower nor a lender be."*

See also **CITATION; PARAPHRASE;** and **PLAGIARISM.**

quote

Quote is a verb that is often misused as a noun. It is incorrect to say, *The essay made use of a witty quote from Proust.* The proper term here is quotation.

R

raise, rear

Traditionally, **raise** in the sense of **bring up** was used exclusively to refer to crops and livestock. *My cousin used to raise chinchillas.* **Rear** was reserved for the bringing up of children. *I was reared by nuns who found me on the porch of the convent.* Few writers continue to observe this distinction.

raise, rise

Raise and **rise** are not different forms of the same verb, but are different verbs. **Raise** is a transitive verb and therefore requires a direct object. *If you raise the light a few inches, we would see better.* **Rise** is an intransitive verb, requiring no direct object. *The old elevator shakes as it rises.* **Rise** is sometimes used colloquially as a noun meaning emotional reaction. *I thought that story would get a rise out of you.* Such usage should be avoided in formal discourse.

rare, scarce

Rare and **scarce** are both used to refer to things that are difficult to get. **Rare** refers to things that are usually valuable. *You have a rare quality of compassion.* **Scarce** generally refers to needed objects that are temporarily in short supply. *Toilet paper was scarce during the revolution.*

rarely ever
The phrase **rarely ever** is redundant, since **rarely** means **infrequently.**

See also **REDUNDANCY.**

rate, register, warrant
Rate is often used casually to mean **deserve** or **have influence.** *You rate highly in our estimation. You rate an ice cream cone for all your help.* **Rate** should not be used in either of these ways in formal writing. **Register** and **warrant** may be used instead. *You register highly in our estimation. You warrant an ice cream cone for all your help.*

ravel, unravel
Ravel and **unravel** are both acceptable terms for describing what happens when woven material comes apart. Either may be used literally or figuratively. **Loosen** and **unloosen,** which, like **ravel** and **unravel,** are synonyms, are not equally acceptable. **Unloosen** should be avoided in formal discourse.

See also **FIGURATIVE LANGUAGE; LITERAL LANGUAGE;** and **LOOSEN, UNLOOSEN.**

real, really
Real is a noun meaning actual. **Really** is an adjective meaning **truly.** **Really** is also used informally as an adjective or adverb meaning **very** or **certainly.** **Real** is often used incorrectly as an adjective or adverb. Such usage should be avoided in formal discourse. Moreover,

really should not be used in formal discourse except to mean **truly.** Use of **really** and **very** for emphasis is casual in contrast to the more formal words, **indeed** and **certainly.**

rear, raise
See also RAISE, REAR.

reason because, reason why
Because should not be used as a relative pronoun with the noun, **reason,** as this is redundant. It is incorrect to say, *The reason is because . . .* The proper relative pronoun is **that.**

Why should not be used as a relative pronoun with the noun, **reason,** for the same reason as **reason because.** It is incorrect to say, *The reason why is . . .* It is sufficient to say, *The reason is . . .*

See also FAULTY PREDICATION.

rebut, refute
Rebut and **refute** both mean **argue against,** but **refute** implies success, carrying the additional meaning of **prove wrong.** *I rebutted her arguments to the best of my abilities, but my own claims were refuted.* **Refute** thus carries a stronger meaning than **rebut.** Stronger still is **confute.**

See also CONFUTE, REFUTE.

recall, recollect, remember
Recall, recollect, and **remember** all mean **thinking again of past events. Remember** often implies effortlessness, while **recall** and **recollect** imply at least a modicum of effort. *When I see you fixing dinner, I re-*

member the war. Do you recollect that I said I don't like sweetbreads?

recant, retract

Both **recant** and **retract** refer to changing one's official statements. **Recant** means **disavow** or **state officially that a previous statement was wrong.** *Many early philosophers were forced to recant when their ideas conflicted with established religious views.* **Retract** means **withdraw a previous statement,** but does not necessarily indicate a change in position. *I retract my accusation at this time, pending further evidence.*

recurrence, reoccurrence

Recurrence may be used to describe an event that has occurred more than twice. *The nightmare's recurrence usually wakes me up.* **Reoccurrence** may be used to describe an event that has occurred a second time. *The first time seemed odd. The reoccurrence seemed uncanny.*

Redundancy

Redundancy is the unnecessary use of different words and/or punctuation to indicate one thing twice. *I like my ant farm better than that of Sandy's.* Here the **'s** to indicate possession is redundant since **that of** already shows to whom the ant farm belongs.

Redundancies

Seldom ever, free gift, old adage, more better, round circle, trite cliché, revert back, repeat again, cancel out, cause to happen, etc.

refer, allude, elude
See also ALLUDE, ELUDE, REFER.

Reference of pronouns
See also PRONOUN REFERENCE.

Reflexive pronouns
Reflexive pronouns are used as object pronouns when they have the same antecedent as the subject. *The investors fooled themselves.* Here, **themselves** is the reflexive pronoun of the subject, **investors.** Some reflexive pronouns are **myself, yourself, himself, ourselves,** and **themselves.** The reflexive pronouns are not inflected to show possession. Thus **theirselves** is an incorrect substitute for **themselves. Hisself** is an incorrect substitute for **himself. Themselves'** is also unacceptable. The proper term is **theirs.**

Reflexive pronouns are sometimes used incorrectly to indicate respect. *This hat belongs to yourself.* There is nothing disrespectful, however, about subject and object case pronouns. Reflexive pronouns should not be used in place of subject or object pronouns.

> *Inappropriate Use of Reflexive Pronouns*
> *I gave the money back to herself. Awards were given to them and myself. I have complete trust in yourself. Themselves are going together.*

See also PRONOUNS.

refute, confute
See also CONFUTE, REFUTE.

refute, rebut
See also **REBUT, REFUTE.**

regard
When used as a noun to show reference, **regard** rather than **regards** should be used in such phrases as **in regard** to or **with regard to. Regards** may be used as a verb as in the phrase **as regards.**

register, rate, warrant
See also **RATE, REGISTER, WARRANT.**

Regular verbs
Regular verbs are verbs whose past tense and past participle end in **-ed** or **-d.**
See also **IRREGULAR VERBS.**

relation of, relation to
Relation of should be used to refer to human relatives. *She is a relation of mine.* **Relation to** should be used for nonhuman relationships. *Surrealist art bears an interesting relation to theories of psychology.*

Relative pronouns
Relative pronouns establish a relationship between a noun and a dependent clause that modifies it. Relative pronouns are **that, which, who, whom,** and **whoever.** *The winner is whoever gets the most ketchup in her ears.*
See also **PRONOUNS.**

relevant, irrelevant
See also **IRRELEVANT, RELEVANT.**

reluctant, reticent

Reluctant means **unwilling.** *I am reluctant to tell you about my investments.* **Reticent** means **quiet** or **unwilling to speak** and is usually used to refer to general character rather than specific situations. *Although he is reticent, he has ways of making his desires known.*

remember, recollect, recall

See also RECALL, RECOLLECT, REMEMBER.

reoccurrence, recurrence

See also RECURRENCE, REOCCURRENCE.

replete, complete

See also COMPLETE, REPLETE.

repress, suppress, oppress

See also OPPRESS, REPRESS, SUPPRESS.

respectful, respective

Respectful is an adjective **meaning full of esteem. Respective** is an adjective meaning **particular.** *We are most respectful of our respective parents.*

restive, restful

Restive means **restless** or **impatient.** *The dog was restive in his new kennel.* **Restful** means **relaxed** or **causing relaxation.** *We had a restful vacation.*

Restrictive clauses and phrases

See also ESSENTIAL CLAUSES AND PHRASES.

reticent, reluctant
See also RELUCTANT, RETICENT.

retract, recant
See also RECANT, RETRACT.

revenge, avenge
See also AVENGE, REVENGE.

reverse, revert
As a verb, **reverse** means **turn and go the opposite way.** It may be used to refer to ideas and policies as well as to physical motion. *The senator reversed his policy on gun control to satisfy his new constituency.* **Revert** means **return to a previously established course.** *If we cannot live safely without guns we may as well revert to living in caves.*

revert back
The phrase **revert back** is redundant since **revert** means **turn back to a former course.**
See also REDUNDANCY.

rise, raise
See also RAISE, RISE.

robbery, burglary
See also BURGLARY, ROBBERY.

Run-on sentences
See also FUSED SENTENCES.

S

's

An apostrophe followed by the letter **s** is sometimes used to show possession and sometimes used in contractions. These two uses are often confused, especially the contraction, **it's** and the possessive pronoun **its**. The **'s** should be used to show possession where nouns are concerned: **the night's darkness, the child's toy.** An **'s** should not be used to show possession where possessive pronouns are concerned: **its aftermath, the marbles are yours.**

An **'s** should be used in the contractions **it's** and **that's.** Use of contractions, however, is inappropriate in formal discourse. The words should be written out, **it is, that is.**

See also **CONTRACTIONS** and **POSSESSIVE CASE.**

Salutations

Salutations appear at the beginning of letters addressing the person to whom they are sent. Informal salutations may be followed by a comma: **Dear Puffy,** and Salutations that are even less formal may be followed by a dash: **Hi ya, Old Chum—.** Formal salutations should be followed by a colon: **To whom it may concern:.**

saw, seen

Saw is the past tense form of the verb **see**. **Seen** is the past participle of the verb **see**. **Seen** is often used incorrectly as the past tense of **see**. In standard English, it is improper to say, *We seen the mail carrier.* It is acceptable, however, to say, *We have seen the mail carrier.*

　　See also **PARTICIPLES**.

scan

Scan can be used to mean **peruse closely** or **peruse hurriedly**. Therefore, the phrases, **scan closely** and **scan hurriedly** are not redundant but are useful in avoiding ambiguity.

scarce, rare

　　See also **RARE, SCARCE**.

seasonable, seasonal

Seasonable means **timely** or **appropriate for the time of year**. *The need for lawn care provides many students with seasonable summer work.* **Seasonal** means **depending on the time of year**. *Business is seasonal in most resort towns.*

Second person

Second person is the form of pronoun and verb that refers to the audience of a discourse. Second person is indicated by the pronoun **you,** and the verb form that agrees with it.

　　See also **PERSON**.

secondly

　　See also **FIRSTLY**.

seen, saw
See also SAW, SEEN.

seldom ever
The phrase **seldom ever** is redundant since **seldom** refers to time. **Ever** should be omitted.

self, subjectivity
Self and **subjectivity** both refer to human individuality. **Subjectivity,** unlike **self,** implies that individuality is an effect produced by social forces operating through language. Since any particular conception of selfhood is an effect produced by language, it is not the inevitable result of being human. **Subjectivity** refers to the self as a social construct.

See also DISCOURSE, LANGUAGE and IDEOLOGY, KNOWLEDGE.

Semantics
Semantics is the area of language pertaining to meaning. The theoretical relationship between semantics and grammar is a subject of scholarly debate. Many believe the rules of grammar should properly be understood as independent of semantics. Others believe semantics informs the most adequate understanding of grammar.

semi, bi
See also BI, SEMI.

Semicolons
Semicolons are marks of punctuation used for separating grammatically equivalent word groups. They can be used for separating two independent clauses that are not

joined by a coordinating conjunction, but whose subjects are too closely related to be separated by a period. *I like your shirt; the color is nice.*

Semicolons can also be used for separating two independent clauses that are related to one another by a conjunctive adverb such as **however, moreover,** and **therefore.** *I like your shirt; however, the fabric looks uncomfortable.*

Semicolons may also be used to separate parts of a list when they consist of word groups that include commas. *Wool, a natural fiber; rayon, a synthetic fiber; and silk, a natural fiber are difficult to iron.*

See also **FAULTY PARALLELISM** and **LISTS.**

sensual, sensuous

Sensual and **sensuous** are adjectives that have come to mean essentially the same thing, having to do with pleasurable sensation. Traditionally, however, **sensual** had a negative connotation associated with sexuality, and **sensuous** had a more positive connotation associated with art. Today this distinction seems dubious, intended to represent certain kinds of physical pleasures as depraved and others as acceptable on experiential, rather than ethical, grounds. Ironically, if **sensuous** has retained its relatively more positive connotation, it has been through association with sexuality as well as with aesthetics.

Sentence fragments

See also **FRAGMENTS.**

Sentence modifiers

A sentence modifier is a word, phrase, or clause used to refer to the sentence as a whole rather than to a particular noun or verb in it. Some sentence modifiers are **apparently, hopefully, it is evident that, perhaps, to my way of thinking,** as well as absolute phrases. Sentence modifiers invariably occur at the beginning of a sentence.

See also ABSOLUTE PHRASE and HOPEFULLY.

Sentence structure

See also SENTENCES.

Sentences

A sentence is a word group consisting of at least one independent clause (containing a subject and a predicate) that is separated from other sentences by an end punctuation mark such as a period. Sentences may be simple, complex, compound, or compound-complex. These different kinds of sentences indicate the kinds of clauses they contain.

Series

A series is a list made up of grammatically equivalent word groups. Members of a series may be separated by commas or by semicolons.

See also COMMAS.

set, sit

Set is a verb meaning **to place** that generally takes a preposition such as **on, in,** or **under** along with a direct object. *She set the shovel on its side.* Sit is a verb meaning **to rest on one's buttocks.** It may or may not take a preposition and should not be used with a direct object other than, in some cases, a reflexive pronoun. *We sit in our hats.*

sex, gender
See also GENDER, SEX.

Sexist language
See also **BIASED LANGUAGE** and **INCLUSIVE LANGUAGE.**

shall, will
Traditionally, complicated distinctions have been observed between the verb forms of **shall** and of **will.** These distinctions have practically disappeared, even in formal discourse. In the past, **shall** was used as a simple expression of intent in the first person, but as an imperative or inevitability in the second and third persons. **Will** was used as an imperative in the first person, but without special emphasis in the second and third persons. More recently, **shall** is used infrequently and interchangeably with **will.**

she/he
See also HE/SHE.

shear, sheer
Shear means **cut.** It is usually used to refer to fleece or hair, but is also used figuratively to refer to power or emotions. *His stare sheared me of my self-possession.* **Sheer** means **swerve.** *As the plane landed, it sheered off the runway.* **Sheer** is also an adjective with two unre-

lated meanings: **extremely thin** and **nearly perpendicular.**

Shifts

Unnecessary shifts in tone, number, person, voice, verb mood, and verb tense should be avoided.

See also **AGREEMENT; CONSISTENCY; MOOD OF VERB;** and **PERSON.**

shrinked

Shrinked is sometimes used improperly as the past tense or past participle of **shrink. Shrinked** is never acceptable in formal writing. The proper past tense form of **shrink** is **shrank.** The past participle is **shrunk.**

Simple future tense

The simple future tense is the verb form indicating that an action is to occur in the future. *We will meet at 7:00.* It is formed by using will as a helping verb along with the main form of the verb.

See also **FUTURE TENSE.**

Simple past tense

The simple past tense is the verb form indicating that an action took place in the past. *We met at 7:00.* Simple past tense is used for relating events that have already taken place.

See also **PAST TENSES.**

Simple present tense

The simple present tense is the verb form indicating an action that takes place in the present or an action that generally or habitually occurs. *We meet at 7:00.* Simple present should be used to describe the action of texts, regardless of what tenses those texts use. *The first chapter of David Copperfield reveals that David was born at midnight.* Here, **reveals** is a simple present tense verb form used for describing what the text says has happened.

See also **PRESENT TENSES.**

Simple sentences

Simple sentences consist of a single independent clause, including a subject and a predicate. *Every action has an equal and opposite reaction.*

simple, simplistic

Simple means uncomplicated. It can be used positively or negatively. *Simple food is often the most healthful.* **Simplistic** means **too simple.** It is always a negative term and is usually applied to ideas or explanations. *His simplistic understanding of justice made it impossible for him to appreciate affirmative action.*

since

Since is a preposition that establishes either a temporal or a logical relationship. It is used with greater precision, however, to refer to temporal relationships.

sit, set

See also SET, SIT.

Slang

Slang is language that is not part of the lexicon of accepted formal discourse. It resembles colloquial speech in that it is informal, but it generally has more recent origins.

Slash

The slash (/) is a punctuation mark used to separate lines of poetry whenever it is not written out in indented verse form. *"Sometimes like a gleaner thou dost keep / Steady thy laden head across a brook"*—Keats. A single space should separate the slash from the word on either side of it.

Slashes also indicate that two or more words are simultaneously applicable: **either/or, her/his, both/ neither.**

slow, slowly

Both **slow** and **slowly** may be used as adverbs. Their use is idiomatic. **Slow** is acceptable in formal writing to refer to watches, trains, and other things that move regularly in time. *My watch is running slow.* **Slowly** is the preferred adverb in most other cases.

smooth, smoothen

Smooth is a transitive verb, taking a direct object. *The polishing machine smoothes the ice before the hockey game.* Here, the direct object of **smooths** is **ice.** **Smoothen** is an intransitive verb, taking no direct object. Thus the only things that can be smoothened are the things that smoothen themselves. *His angry face smoothened into a look of curiosity.*

See also **DIRECT OBJECT, INTRANSITIVE VERBS,** and **TRANSITIVE VERBS.**

sneaked, snuck

Properly, the past tense and past participle form of the verb **sneak** is **sneaked,** not **snuck.** **Snuck** is sometimes used in casual speech but should be avoided in formal writing.

so

So is a coordinating conjunction and should not be used for emphasis without correlation. It is incorrect to say, *Your children are so ugly.* The conjunction requires further explanation of how ugly the children are. *Your children are so ugly that they've never tasted milk that wasn't spoiled.*

so . . . as, as . . . as

See also AS . . . AS, SO . . . AS.

some and verb

See also COLLECTIVE NOUNS and INDEFINITE PRONOUNS.

sort, kind, type

See also KIND, SORT, TYPE.

sound

Sound may be used as a linking verb connecting the subject with the subject complement. The subject complement should not be an adverb. *You sound bad. The test sounds difficult.* **Sound** may also be used as a verb that takes an adverb. *The gong sounds mysteriously.*

See also LINKING VERBS and SUBJECT COMPLEMENTS.

Specialized language
See also JARGON.

Specific terms
Specific terms differ in degree from more general terms. **Pea** is more specific a term than **vegetable,** but less specific than **sweet pea.** Specific terms are often more desirable than general terms because they are more precise and supply more detail. General terms, however, may be preferable to specific terms if specific terms add details that are unimportant to the subject at hand.

> *Specific vs. General Terms*
> *Boy, person; poodle, dog; dog, animal; animal, living thing; accident, event; falling down, accident; slipping on a banana peel, falling down*

See also GENERAL TERMS.

spell out
Spell out is acceptable in formal writing, but **spell out the details** and **spell out the particulars** are redundant phrases.

See also REDUNDANCY.

Spelling
The spelling of English words has been normalized since the eighteenth century. Inconsistent and irregular spelling should be avoided. Some differences in accepted spelling exist between British and American English for words such as **color/colour** and **center/centre.**

Split infinitives

Infinitives are main verb forms preceded by the preposition **to.** Many grammarians object to the splitting of infinitives by other words and word groups, although split infinitives are often considered acceptable. *How can you hope to ever get rich if you insist on being nice to people?* Here the infinitive, **to get,** is split by the adverb, **ever.** The sentence may be rewritten, *How can you hope ever to get rich . . . if you insist on being nice to people?*

> *Split Infinitives*
> *We are required to now give blood. I want to only rest a while. I have known you to never walk away from a fight. They love to seemingly care about others.*

See also **INFINITIVES.**

Squinting modifier

A squinting modifier is an adjective or adverb that ambiguously seems to modify the words before and after it. *The views I held firmly convinced the others.* Here, **firmly** could be taken to modify either **held** or **convinced.** This kind of ambiguity should be avoided. The example could be rewritten: *The views I firmly held convinced the others,* or, *The views I held convinced the others firmly.*

See also **MODIFIERS.**

stalactite, stalagmite

Stalactites and stalagmites are cone-shaped mineral formations found in caves. Stalactites hang downward from the cave's ceiling; stalagmites rise upward from the floor.

Standard English

Standard English is a literary, or written, language that has developed over centuries through attempts to regulate the spelling, grammar, and usage of written English in order to promote clarity and consistency. Although its rules have changed over the years, these rules have evolved more slowly than the rules governing spoken English, which tends to be less consistent and less capable of articulating complex ideas with precision.

See also CONSISTENCY and FORMALITY.

statistics

Statistics, like many other words ending in **-ics** may be either a plural or a singular noun. When used generally, to refer to an art or study, **statistics** is singular and takes a singular verb. *Statistics is a notoriously boring class.* When used specifically to refer to particular examples, **statistics** is plural and takes a plural verb. *These statistics are misleading.*

See also -ICS.

stayed, stood

Stood is often used colloquially instead of **stayed** to mean **remained.** In formal writing, **stood** should not be used as a synonym for **remained.** Thus it is inappropriate to say, *I continued on while the others stood at the hotel.* The appropriate term here is **stayed.**

stood, stayed

See also STAYED, STOOD.

strata, stratum

Strata is the plural of **stratum**. **Stratas** is nonstandard and should be avoided.

Subject

The subject of a sentence is that which carries out the action described by the predicate. The complete subject includes a noun and any of its modifiers. In the sentence, *Everyone who had any sense left the room*, **everyone** is the subject and **everyone who had any sense** is the complete subject.

Subject case

The subject case is the pronoun case indicating that which carries out an action described by the verb. Personal pronouns in the subject case are **I, you, she, he, it, they,** and **we.**

See also **PERSONAL PRONOUNS** and **PRONOUN CASES.**

Subject complements

The subject complement occurs after a linking verb and describes or restates the subject. It can be a noun or a pronoun. *The mysterious lump was I.* Notice that if the subject complement is a personal pronoun, the pronoun takes the subject case even though it appears after the verb.

> *Faulty Subject Complements*
> *The killer seemed to be him. It sounded like them. The hardest worker turned out to be her. Do you feel like me?*

See also **COMPLEMENT; PRONOUN CASES;** and **SUBJECT CASE.**

Subject-verb agreement

Subjects and verbs must agree in number. Singular nouns take singular verbs and plural nouns take verbs with a corresponding plural form.

Subject-verb agreement in Black English differs from standard English. Indeed, this difference is perhaps the most obvious distinction between the two dialects.

> *Faulty Agreement: Subject-Verb*
> *I considers, you exclaims, she possess, they disintegrates, we prefers*

> *Correct Agreement: Subject-Verb*
> *I eliminate, you condone, he establishes, they elevate, we conceive*

Note that special subject-verb agreement problems are posed by sentences that use collective nouns as subjects:

> *Faulty agreement: Collective Noun-Verb*
> *nothing are, the batch are done, the group decide*

> *Correct Agreement: Collective Noun-Verb*
> *the committee thinks, the herd stampedes, all members of the group decide*

See also AGREEMENT; BLACK ENGLISH; COLLECTIVE NOUNS; and CONSISTENCY.

Subjunctive mood

One of the three verb moods, the others are (the declarative mood and the imperative mood), the subjunctive mood indicates that an action is conditional or speculative. *Should there be no more paper clips, you can use safety pins.* Here the conditional verb, **be** takes the subjunctive mood.

Faulty Subjunctive

If I was wealthy; even if you have time; the sun be shining now

Correct Subjunctive

If I had the money; if such be your preference; if he were shorter

See also CONDITIONAL SENTENCES and MOOD OF VERB.

Subordinate clauses

See also DEPENDENT CLAUSES.

Subordinating conjunctions

Subordinating conjunctions turn independent clauses into dependent clauses and join them in a logical relationship with a different independent clause. Subordinating conjunctions are **after, although, as, because, before, even, if, once, since, though, unless, until, when,** and **while.** *Honk if you are tired of noise pollution.* Here the subordinating conjunction **if** turns the clause **you are tired of noise pollution** into a dependent clause and relates it to the independent clause **honk.**

See also CONJUNCTIONS and SUBORDINATION.

Subordination

Subordination is a way of relating the ideas in different clauses by showing that one clause depends on or is less important than the other clause. Clauses are subordinated to other clauses by means of subordinating conjunctions.

See also SUBORDINATING CONJUNCTIONS.

such

Such, like **so,** is a coordinating conjunction that should not be used for emphasis without correlation. It is incorrect to say, *I have such a problem with my back.* More information is required explaining how much of a problem exists. The sentence should read, *I have such a problem with my back that the rest of my body has agreed to ignore it completely.*

See also **AS, LIKE.**

Suffixes

Suffixes are letters added onto the ends of words that change them into different words. Some suffixes are **-ous, -ity, -able,** and -ness. Few suffixes require hyphens to separate them from the stem of the word. One suffix that does require a hyphen is **-elect.**

See also **COMBINING FORMS.**

Superlative form

Superlative form is the comparative form of an adjective or adverb that identifies a noun or verb as an extreme among all other like examples. *I am the tallest person in the room.* Here **tallest** is a superlative adjective. Other comparative forms are positive and comparative.

See also **ADJECTIVES, ADVERBS,** and **COMPARISON.**

suppose

When **suppose** is used in the passive voice, it should take the past tense form, **supposed.** *We are supposed to arrive at eight.* **Supposed** in this construction is often used to mean **required.** Properly, however, it is even milder than **expected,** meaning simply **thought.**

See also PASSIVE VOICE.

suppress, repress, oppress

See also OPPRESS, REPRESS, SUPPRESS.

sure

Sure is properly used as an adjective to modify nouns. *Snow is a sure sign of cold weather.* The adverb form of **sure** is **surely.** Frequently, **sure** is used incorrectly as an adverb instead of surely. *I sure am fascinated.* Here **sure** is used incorrectly to modify the verb, **am.**

sympathy, empathy

See also EMPATHY, SYMPATHY.

Syntax

Syntax refers to the way words are put together in groups and in sequence. A problem in syntax is a problem in grammatical structure, as opposed to inflection (word forms), and semantics (meaning).

T

Tag questions
Tag questions are words that repeat a question that has just been asked in different words or that rephrases a statement that has just been made as a question. *You don't like raw sewage, do you?* Here, **do you?** is a tag question.

take, bring
See also BRING, TAKE.

take place, occur
See also OCCUR, TAKE PLACE.

Tautology
See also REDUNDANCY.

Technical terms
See also JARGON.

temerity, timidity
Temerity means **boldness.** *Everyone is embarrassed by your sexual temerity with the opposite sex.* **Timidity,** of course, means just the opposite. *Everyone is disappointed by your timidity with the opposite sex.*

tend to

Tend to is often used informally instead of **attend to.** Only **attend to** is appropriate in formal writing to mean **pay attention to.**

Tenses

Tenses are verb forms that indicate when an action takes place. The tenses are simple past, simple present, simple future, past perfect, present perfect, future perfect, past progressive, present progressive, future progressive, past perfect progressive, present perfect progressive, and future perfect progressive.

than, then

Than is a conjunction used to compare two things. *We are bigger than they are.* **Then** is an adverb or noun that refers to a point in the past or the future. *First we sow, then we reap.*

The grammatical problem known as incomplete comparisons often occurs in sentences that use the word **than.** *Gervis is taller when he wears his new shoes than his sneakers.* Here the phrases, **when he wears his new shoes** and **his sneakers** are misleadingly compared. The sentence should be revised to read, *Gervis is taller when he wears his new shoes than when he wears his sneakers.*

See also **INCOMPLETE COMPARISON.**

that, which

That should be used to introduce essential clauses and phrases; **which** should be used to introduce nonessential clauses and phrases. *All the bushes that have been* *trimmed look phony. The bushes, which don't grow very large, look better untended.* In general, clauses and phrases introduced by **which** should be set off from the rest of a sentence by commas. Clauses and phrases introduced by **that** should not be set off by commas.

See also ESSENTIAL CLAUSES AND PHRASES.

their, there, they're

Their is a possessive personal pronoun, **there** indicates a location, and **they're** is a contraction of **they are.** These words are often confused. *They're putting their coats there.*

theirselves

Theirselves is a nonstandard reflexive personal pronoun whose proper form in standard English is **themselves.**

See also REFLEXIVE PRONOUNS.

then, than

See also THAN, THEN.

there is/are

There can take either a plural or a singular verb depending on whether the noun it refers to is singular or plural. *There is a big Jell-O salad on my desk. There are many banana slices in it.* If **there** modifies a collective noun, the verb may be either singular or plural. *There are a lot of grapes, too.* Here, **are** could be said to refer to the plural, **grapes.** *There is a lot of grapes.* Here, **is** could be said to refer to the singular **lot.**

See also COLLECTIVE NOUNS.

Thesis

A thesis is the main claim or assertion made by a piece of expository writing. It should appear near the beginning of the work. It should comprehend the points made in the work that follows; that is, all the ideas discussed in a piece of writing should be related to the thesis. Conversely, however, the thesis should not be so broad that it comprehends ideas not discussed in the work.

A thesis is original when it makes a claim about other writings or other claims. Otherwise it merely presents facts or summarizes opinions.

See also ATTRIBUTION; FOCUS; and ORIGINALITY.

Third person

Third person is the form of verbs and pronouns that refer to their subjects as being neither the speaker or writer nor the audience. *He lived in Guatemala.* Here, **he** is a third person pronoun.

See also PERSON.

thirdly

See also FIRSTLY.

this and reference

This is often used vaguely to refer to complicated sentences and paragraphs rather than to particular concepts. Such vague reference should be avoided.

See also PRONOUN REFERENCE.

this here
This here is sometimes used colloquially instead of **this**. **This here** is redundant and should be avoided in formal writing.

though
Though is often used informally as an adverb at the end of a sentence rather than as a conjunction at the beginning or in the middle. Such usage should be avoided in formal writing. *We arrived early. We didn't stay long, though.* In formal writing, **however** is a more appropriate term.

See also CONJUNCTIONS.

thus, thusly
Thusly is an incorrect form of **thus**. **Thus** means **therefore** or **as a result** and never takes the adverb form.

'til, till, until
'Til is no longer an acceptable term. **Till** and **until** are both acceptable and may be used interchangeably. **Until,** however, is usually preferred at the beginning of a sentence.

timidity, temerity
See also TEMERITY, TIMIDITY.

to, too, two
These homonyms are often confused in written discourse. **To** is a preposition used with verbs such as **come, listen,** and before main verbs to form the infinitive, as in **to soften. Too** means **also; two** is the number.

Tone

Tone consists of all of the features of written and spoken discourse that indicate the attitude of the speaker or writer. Although tone can be described in many ways, it is often most useful to distinguish between a formal and a casual tone. A formal tone can be achieved by avoiding colloquial terms and nonstandard grammatical constructions.

See also FORMALITY.

tortuous, torturous

These words have distinct meanings but are often confused. **Tortuous** means **twisted, winding,** or **convoluted.** It may be used to refer to mental situations as well as to physical things. *I could not follow your tortuous reasoning.* **Torturous** means **capable of inflicting excruciating pain.** *The waves dragged him across the torturous barnacles.*

toward, towards

Both **toward** and **towards** are acceptable, but **toward** is preferred.

Trademarks

Trademarks are proper nouns and should be capitalized: **EZ Haul, Jiffy Spin, Slop N Good.**

Transitions

Transitions are logical connections made between one idea and another. Depending on the complexity of the ideas to be connected, transitions may consist of a few words or several paragraphs. Strong transitions explain fully and concisely what two ideas have to do with each other and what the significance is when they are considered together. Weak transitions merely indicate additional information without showing how the new information relates to what has already been said. Weak transitions are often accomplished with **and, also, moreover,** and **furthermore.** Such words suggest that a discussion consists of a simple list of concepts and are appropriate only when the writer's aim is simply to amass information. Most writing, however, requires that emphasis be apportioned carefully among various ideas, that qualifications be made, and that complicated ideas be explained and restated in different contexts. Most meaningful transitions use key words from both portions of text to be related, bringing them together in sentences that explain their relationship.

See also **KEY WORDS** and **PRONOUN REFERENCE.**

Transitive verbs

Transitive verbs indicate that an action is carried out by a subject on its object. *She smoothed the wet concrete.* Here **smoothed** is a transitive verb taking **wet concrete** as its object.

Intransitive verbs are sometimes used incorrectly as transitive verbs. *The coach evolved his team.*

> ### Incorrect Transitive Verbs
> *The boss resigned his employee. The artist emerged his new painting. He languished his tennis game. The students blossomed their abilities.*

See also **INTRANSITIVE VERBS** and **LINKING VERBS.**

Trite expressions

See also **CLICHÉS.**

try and, try to
The expression **try and** as in, *Try and find the neigh-bors' pet viper,* is less precise than **try to** and should be avoided in formal writing.

type, kind, sort
　See also KIND, SORT, TYPE.

U

Underline

The underline, like italics, is used to indicate the title of a book-length written work or film. It may also be used for emphasis in place of italics. *Do you <u>know</u> they will arrive tomorrow?*

See also EMPHASIS.

undoubtedly, doubtless

See also DOUBTLESS, NO DOUBT, UNDOUBTEDLY.

uninterested, disinterested

See also DISINTERESTED, UNINTERESTED.

unique

Unique is an absolute term meaning one of a kind. It should not be used in comparisons as in the phrases, **more unique, extremely unique,** or **as unique as.**

See also ABSOLUTE TERMS.

unloosen, loosen

See also LOOSEN, UNLOOSEN.

unravel, ravel

See also RAVEL, UNRAVEL.

us, we

We is a personal pronoun in the subject case; **us** is the object case of the same pronoun. In formal prose, **we** should be used whenever the pronoun carries out the action indicated by the verb, regardless of where it occurs in the sentence. *They are not so desperate as we.* **Us** should be used whenever the pronoun receives the action indicated by the verb. *Do not mess with us.*

See also **OBJECT CASE** and **SUBJECT CASE.**

use to, used to

Use to is often incorrect, since the phrase usually identifies an action that took place in the past. The past tense form, **used to** should be used. In sixteenth-century England, **use to** used to be an acceptable way of saying **habitually.** *We use to smoke tobacco after dinner.* This usage is now obsolete. Today, **use to** should only be used in sentences in which the past participle is rendered inappropriate by the helping verb **did.** *We did use to know them.*

V

valuable, invaluable
See also INVALUABLE, VALUABLE.

various
Various is sometimes followed by the preposition **of** in casual speech. *Various of your marbles are lost.* **Of** should not be used after **various** in formal writing. This sentence may be rewritten: *You have various missing marbles,* or, *You have lost various marbles,* or, *A variety of your marbles are lost.*

venal, venial
Venal means **morally corrupt.** *The practice of using professional connections to do special favors for friends is regarded as venal by some societies but is acceptable by others.* **Venial** means **morally wrong, but excusable.** Traditionally, the word has been used as a religious term to distinguish between sins for which one went to hell and those for which one was not necessarily damned. It may be used, however, to refer to any mistake that is somewhat, but not especially, bad. *Forgetting to pick up the dry cleaning was a venial sin. Forgetting to pick up Uncle Fred was unpardonable.*

Verb agreement

Verbs must agree with their subjects in person, number, and mood.

See also **AGREEMENT; AMOUNT, NUMBER; MOOD OF VERB;** and **PERSON.**

Verbals

See also **VERBAL PHRASES.**

Verb conjugation

Verb conjugation is the array of inflection of the forms of a verb for tense, person, and number.

See also **AGREEMENT; PERSON;** and **TENSES.**

Verb mood

See also **MOOD OF VERB.**

Verb tenses

See also **TENSES.**

Verb voice

Verb voice indicates whether an action is active or passive.

See also **ACTIVE VOICE** and **PASSIVE VOICE.**

Verbal phrases

Verbal phrases are phrases based on verbs that are used as nouns or modifiers. They may be gerund phrases, infinitive phrases, or participial phrases. *I hate what you did to the living room.* Here, **to the living room** is an infinitive verbal phrase.

See also **GERUNDS, INFINITIVES,** and **PARTICIPIAL PHRASES.**

Verbs

Verbs are the parts of speech that indicate action. Verb forms are inflected for tense, mood, person, and number. They may be transitive, intransitive, or linking, depending on whether the subject acts on an object and on whether the subject has a complement. Verbs may take the active or the passive voice. Verbs may be used in phrases and clauses that act as nouns, adjectives, or adverbs. Such verbal phrases are also known as verbals. They may be infinitive phrases, gerund phrases, or participial phrases. Verbs that modify other verbs are known as helping verbs.

Verbs may be regular or irregular depending on how they are conjugated, and on how their forms vary from the main form of the verb.

See also ACTIVE VOICE; GERUNDS; HELPING VERBS; INFINITIVES; INTRANSITIVE VERBS; IRREGULAR VERBS; LINKING VERBS; MOOD OF VERB; PASSIVE VOICE; REGULAR VERBS; TRANSITIVE VERBS; and VERBAL PHRASES.

virtually, practically

See also PRACTICALLY, VIRTUALLY.

Vocabulary

Vocabulary is the knowledge of words and their meanings. A good vocabulary is necessary for writing well. A good way to develop one's vocabulary is by reading a variety of books and other writings.

W

wait for, wait on

Wait on is often used informally instead of **wait for**. In formal writing, **wait on** is appropriate only as a synonym for **serve**. **Wait for** is the appropriate phrase to use in the sense of **await**.

wake, waken, awake, awaken

See also AWAKE, AWAKEN, WAKE, WAKEN.

want, want for

Want for is acceptable instead of **want** only when need is an intended meaning. *You will want for food if you don't go to the store.* **Want** should be used to indicate **desire**. *I don't want to go to the store.*

warrant, rate, register

See also RATE, REGISTER, WARRANT.

way, ways

Ways should not be used instead of **way** in formal writing. *They came from a long way off.*

whence

See also FROM WHENCE.

where. . . at

It is nonstandard to use the preposition **at** with **where,** and it is unacceptable in formal writing. *Where is the Guggenheim Museum at?* This question should read, *Where is the Guggenheim Museum?*

which, that

See also THAT, WHICH.

while

While is used to refer to periods of time. Otherwise, it may be used as a synonym for **whereas** or **although,** but one of these other words is generally preferable in formal writing.

who, whom

Who is a personal pronoun in the subject case. **Whom** is the object case of the same pronoun. Traditionally, **whom** has been used whenever the pronoun receives the action of the verb, regardless of where it appears in the sentence. *To whom do you wish to speak? I do not know the party to whom you refer. I don't know whom you mean.* The use of **who** instead of **whom** as an object case pronoun has been steadily increasing and is no longer considered as inappropriate as it once was.

See also PRONOUN CASES and SUBJUNCTIVE MOOD.

who's, whose

Who's is a contraction of **who is.** It should not be confused with the possessive personal pronoun **whose.** *Whose dirty socks are these?* Contrast *Who's at the* *door?* This sentence is grammatically correct, although use of contractions is too casual for formal writing.

See also **POSSESSIVE CASE.**

Word choice

See also **DICTION.**

Wordiness

Wordiness is a problem in writing caused by inflated diction or lack of conciseness.

See also **CONCISENESS** and **INFLATED DICTION.**

wreak, wreck,

Wreak is a word that is nearly obsolete except in the case of the phrase **wreak havoc** where it means **inflict.** It should not be confused with **wreck** which means **destroy.** Neither **wreak** nor **wreck** should be confused with **reek**, qhich refers to a strong, unpleasant smell.

Wrong words

Wrong words are words used incorrectly. Their repeated use may result from a weak vocabulary combined with an attempt to disguise a lack of knowledge with inflated diction.

See also **INFLATED DICTION** and **VOCABULARY.**

Y

your, you're

Your and **you're** are often confused. **Your** is a possessive personal pronoun. *Your dog is on fire.* **You're** is a contraction of **you are.** *You're a careless smoker.* **You're** is acceptable in casual writing. In formal writing, contractions should be avoided.

yourself

Yourself should be used only as a reflexive pronoun. *How can you live with yourself?* **Yourself** should not be used instead of **you** either as a subject or object. Thus, it is incorrect to say, *I will give the mice to Dave and yourself.* **You** is the appropriate term here.

See also **REFLEXIVE PRONOUNS.**

INFORMATIVE AND
FUN READING

__THE RAINFOREST BOOK by Scott Lewis
   Preface by Robert Redford   0-425-13769-4/$3.99
Look into the spectacular world of tropical rainforests--their amazing
diversity, the threats to their survival, and the ways we can preserve them
for future generations. This easy-to-read handbook is full of practical tips
for turning your concern for rainforests into action.

__MOTHER NATURE'S GREATEST HITS
   by Bartleby Nash   0-425-13652-3/$4.50
Meet the animal kingdom's weirdest, wackiest, wildest creatures! Learn
about dancing badgers, beer-drinking raccoons, 180-foot worms, Good
Samaritan animals and more!

__FOR KIDS WHO LOVE ANIMALS by Linda Koebner
with the ASPCA   0-425-13632-9/$4.50
Where and how do animals live? How did they evolve? Why are they
endangered? Explore the wonders of the animal kingdom while you
discover how to make the Earth a safer home for all animals.

__SAFE FOOD by Michael F. Jacobson, Ph.D., Lisa Y.
Lefferts and Anne Witte Garland 0-425-13621-3/$4.99
 This clear, helpful guide explains how you can avoid hidden hazards--and
shows that eating safely doesn't have to mean hassles, high prices, and
special trips to health food stores.